A GRIMOIRE OF T
Volume 3. Psalm

Dr. Lazarus Corbeaux
2019

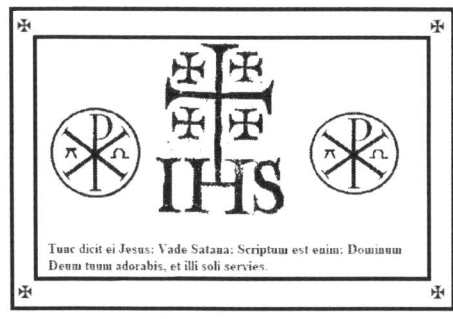

COPYRIGHT & DISCLAIMER

A Grimoire of the Psalms Volume 3. Psalms 101-150

© 2019 Laci Metheny

No part of this book may be reproduced in any written, electronic, recording, or photocopying without the written permission of the author.

This book is not intended as a substitute for medical, legal, or any other professional advice. The reader should regularly consult a physician in regards to the matter of his/her health and particularly in regards to any symptoms that may require diagnosis and medical attention. The reader should also consult licensed legal professionals in regards to any matters of the law, whether criminal or civil. Neither the author nor the publishers assume any liability for the use, or misuse, of any of the information provided in this text. It is presented as an academic study of folklore, and neither the author nor the publisher will assume any liability for damages of any kind, that may result from the use of the information presented here.

CONTACT

Facebook:
http://www.facebook.com/drcorbeauxsconjurerom

Wordpress:
http://www.drcorbeaux.wordpress.com

Youtube:
http://www.youtube.com/user/thetoadsbool

Email: drcorbeaux@gmail.com

+BMN+ATD+OFYL+
Amen
+++
I
N
R
I
I N R I + I N R I
I
N
R
I

INRI✠OW✠C✠T✠B✠SB✠W✠IHVH

A NOTE ON THE TEXT

The order of the Psalms will be based upon the King James Version of the Bible, as it is the most widespread, so to use this text you will need either a KJV Bible or one of the small New Testaments that contain the Book of Psalms.

The Psalm number will be presented in the left hand corner, followed by the specific seals, talismans, and workings that relate to that Psalm.

May God bless you in your work,
Dr. Lazarus Corbeaux
+++

PSALM 101

FOR ATTRACTION

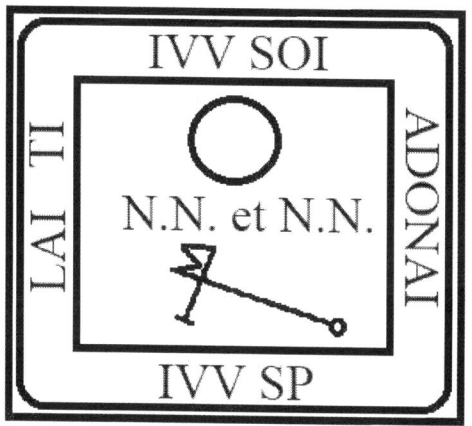

Mark the above seal on copper during the Day and Hour of Venus, with the moon increasing. Fumigate it with rose, and anoint it with pure olive oil, while praying the psalm over it seven times. Replace N.N. et N.N. with your name and your target's name respectively. Wear the seal near your heart when you are around them. At night, sleep with the seal under your pillow.

TO MAKE A PERSON HONEST

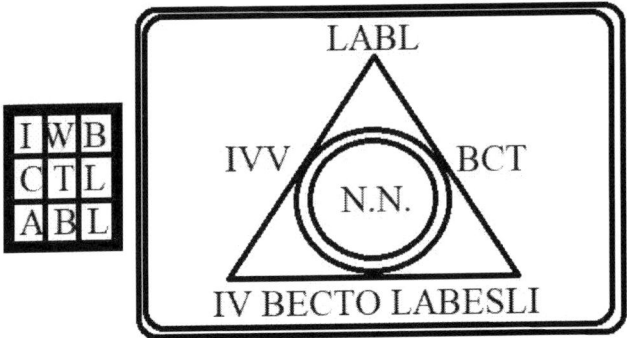

Mark the above seal on tin, replacing N.N. with the target's name, and draw the magic square on the back. Fumigate it with cedar and frankincense, while praying the psalm over it three times. Do this every day for nine days, and bury the seal at the east side of a church.

FOR FIDELITY

Mark the above seal on copper during the Day and Hour of Venus and fumigate it with hemp and magnolia. Pray the psalm seven times over it and wrap it in green cloth with some of your hair and your spouse's hair. Hide the seal within your mattress.

TO KEEP WICKED PEOPLE AWAY

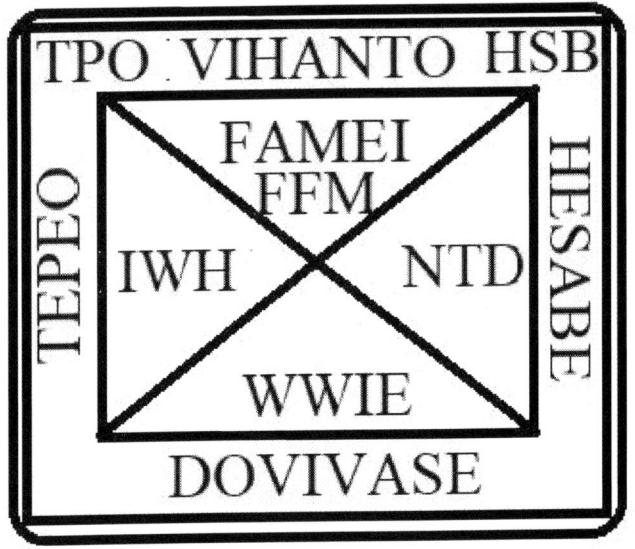

Mark the above seal on clean parchment in iron gall ink. Carry the seal sewn into red cloth with a small piece of mirror. Fumigate this with peppercorns while praying the psalm five times.

TO STOP SLANDER

Mark the above seal in black ink on a mirror's surface during the last night of the moon. Catch the reflection of the moon within the center of the seal and pray the psalm nine times. Fumigate the mirror with camphor, and hang the mirror above your bed.

PSALM 102

TO OBTAIN HELP FROM ANOTHER

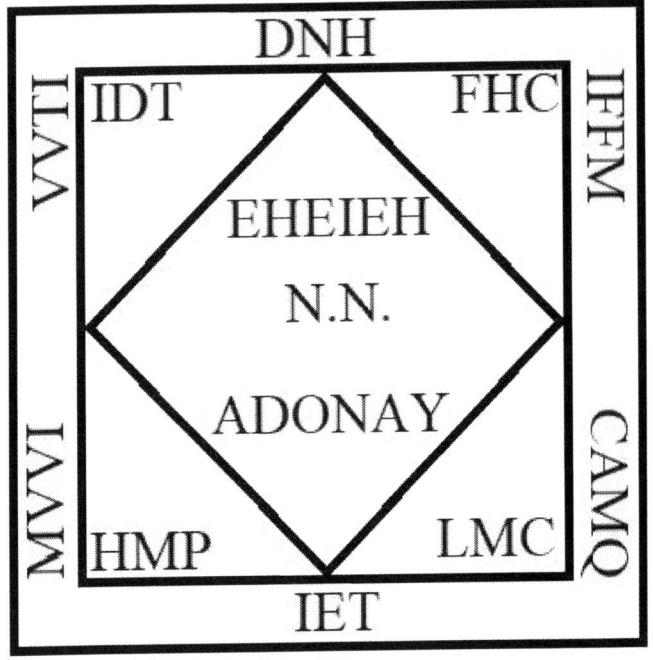

Mark the above seal on clean parchment using green ink on a Friday at 3:00pm, replacing N.N. with the name of the target.. Keep the seal in a small pouch with a piece of amber and pray the psalm seven times over it, reciting the name of the person from whom you seek help seven times after each recitation. Wear it near your heart until the help has been granted.

TO MAKE SOMEONE DESPISED

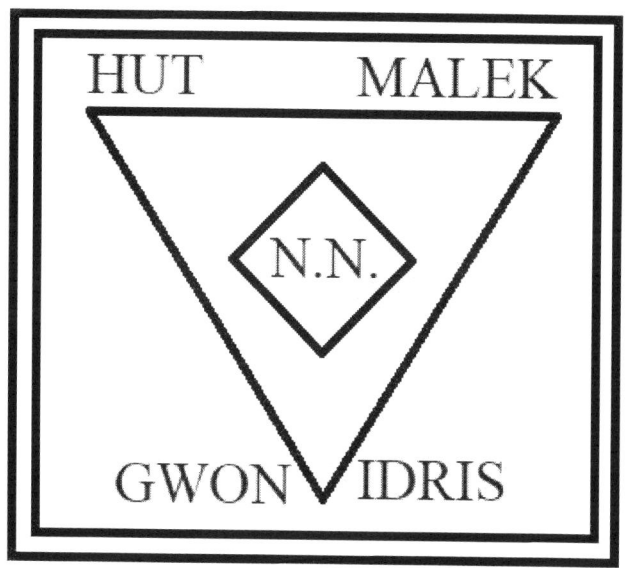

"EHEIEH LAO, LOAT, DAR"

Obtain holy water from a church on Good Friday and take it to a cemetery. Clear a patch of dirt, and use the holy water to smooth it out. With a stick, draw the above seal directly on the dirt, while reciting the words "EHEIEH, LAO, LOAT, DAR." Replace N.N. with the person's name and pray the psalm nine times over the patch of dirt. After this has been done, cover the spot with sticks and leaves.

TO MAKE AN ALCOHOLIC SUFFER

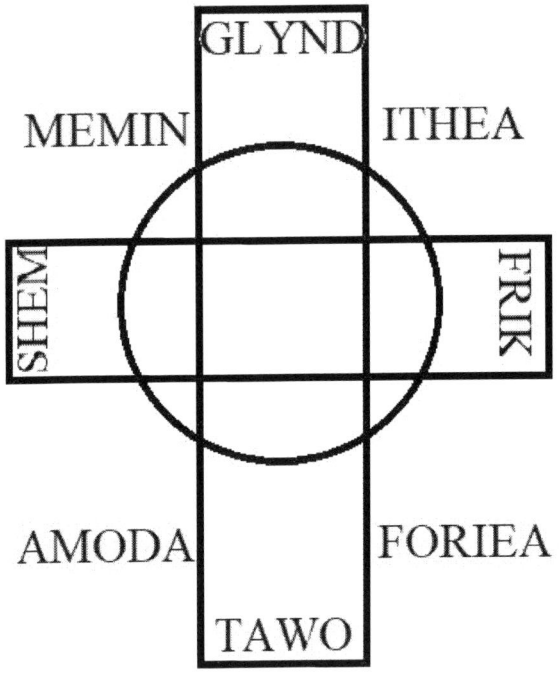

Make the above seal on clean parchment with iron gall ink, mixed with a pinch of copper sulfate. On a Wednesday at 1:00am, place a bottle of the target's favorite liquor on top of the seal and pray the psalm six times, reciting the words of the seal three times after each recitation. Give the liquor to the person as a gift.

TO RECOVER AND REBUILD

On a Monday when the moon is in first quarter, mark the above seal on a plate of silver and fumigate it with willow bark while praying the psalm three times. With a brass nail, consecrated with holy water, olive oil, and the Lord's prayer three times;, attach the seal above your door, driving the nail through the O in ZION.

PSALM 103

FOR HEALING OF THE BODY

Mark the above talisman on clean parchment that has been consecrated by being present at the elevation of the host at a Mass. Pray the psalm 3, 9, or 33 times over the talisman, depending on the severity of the illness, and sew it up in red silk. Hang this around the neck of the patient.

TO RESTORE YOUTH

SID GVRTEL
DIS LETRVG
IDS TREGVL
F.F.F.

Write the above words on a plate with blood from your left ring finger. Pray the psalm seven times over the plate on a Friday with the moon waxing. Pour holy water gathered during a Sunday mass and wash your face with it.

TO RESTORE FRIENDSHIP

HEV NAS ANV HAHYAV
H　　　　N.N.　　　　V
HEV NAS ANV HAHYAV

On the first Sunday of the month, when the bell rings for morning mass, write the above talisman on clean parchment with red ink, using a goose feather quill. Replace N.N. with the name of the person you wish friendship restored with. Pray the psalm three times over it, and burn the seal to ashes with flame from a white candle. Powder the ashes and place them in your navel.

PSALM 104

TO RAISE LIGHTNING

Make the above seal on iron on Monday in the hour of Mars with the moon waxing. Pray the psalm 5 times over it, fumigating it with peppercorns. To invoke the seal, heat it while praying the psalm five times, then drop it in a basin of water directly under the sky.

TO BANISH A STORM

Mark the above seal on birch bark with red ink and pray the psalm four times over it. Fumigate it with frankincense. Burn the seal in the open air.

PROTECTION FROM EARTHQUAKE

Mark the above seal on lead during a solar eclipse. Fumigate it with myrrh and cedar and pray the psalm nine times over it. Nail it to the beams of the building you wish protected.

TO BANISH FLOODWATERS

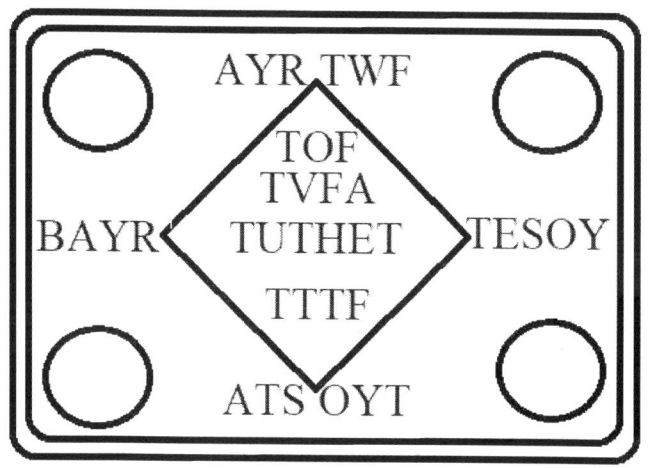

Mark the above seal five times on clean parchment. Fumigate it with camphor while praying the psalm three times. Cast the seals, one at a time, into the waters, while reciting the words **ADONAY, ELOHIM, CONSUMMATUM EST. FIAT FIAT FIAT.**

TO DRAW BIRDS

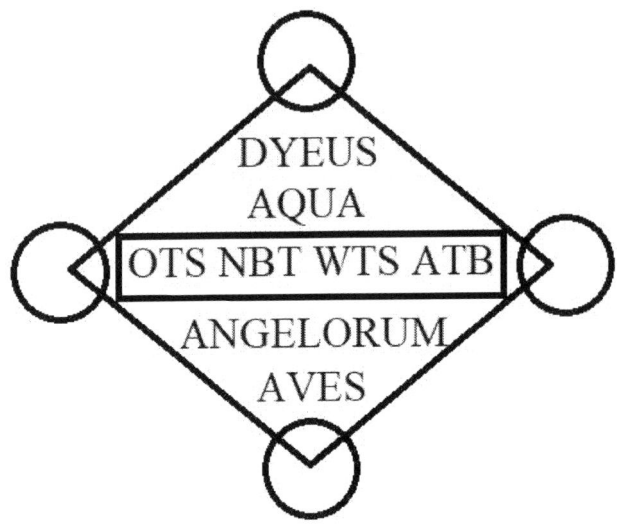

Mark the above seal on the bottom of a white bowl with blue ink. Fumigate it with burning wheat and pray the psalm over it devoutly. Pour spring water into the bowl, and sprinkle the water around the area to be affected.

FOR ABUNDANT GRASS AND HAY

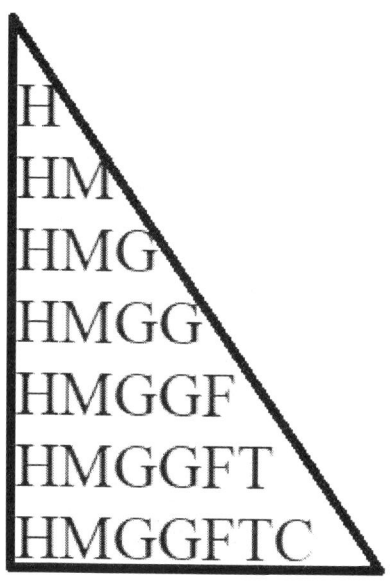

Mark the above seal on clean parchment in the blood of a red rooster. Fumigate it with a twig from a bird's nest and a bluejay feather while praying the psalm over it seven times. Bury the seal in the middle of your field.

PSALM 105

TO MAKE A PERSON'S DEEDS KNOWN

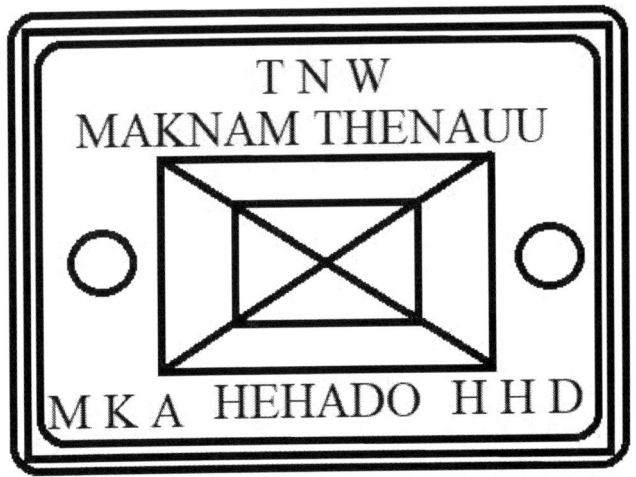

Mark the above seal on nine clean pieces of parchment during a full moon. Afterwards, consecrate each seal by reciting the psalm three times over each. At dawn on a Wednesday, burn the seals to ash and mix them with dirt from the east, west, north, and south sides of a church. Throw the mixture on the person's doorstep.

TO MAKE A PERSON KEEP THEIR PROMISES

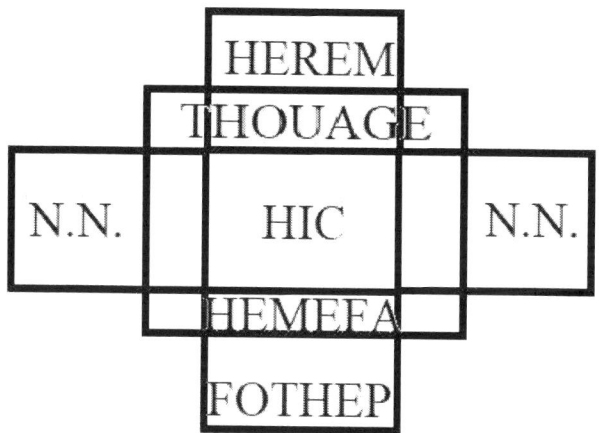

Mark the above seal on a new white plate, replacing N.N. and N.N. with your name, and the name of the individual you wish to enchant. On top of this plate, burn an olive oil lamp and pray the psalm seven times, in honor of the seven spirits that minister around the throne of God. Allow the lamp to burn out. Afterwards, wrap the plate in green cloth and hide it in a high place of your home.

PROTECTION FROM THE POWERFUL

Mark the above words on twelve slips of parchment, in honor of the 12 Holy Apostles of the Lord. Fumigate the seals with frankincense and myrrh and reduce the seals to ashes. Carry these ashes in a small vial around the neck and pray the psalm three times before bed each night, while holding the vial in your left hand.

TO DESTROY SOMEONE'S PROSPERITY

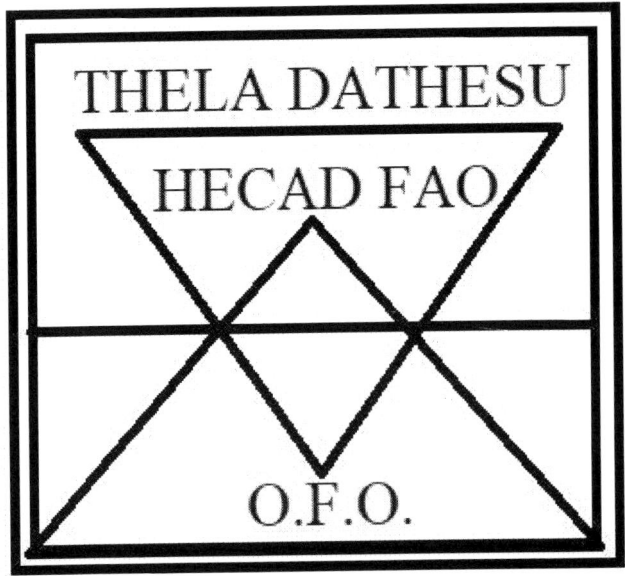

Mark the above seal in lead on a Saturday during the hour of Saturn, the moon decreasing, Pray the psalm nine times over it, fumigating it with patchouli and sulfur. Bury the seal on the person's property.

TO CAUSE MISFORTUNE UNTIL A PERSON DOES AS THEY ARE TOLD

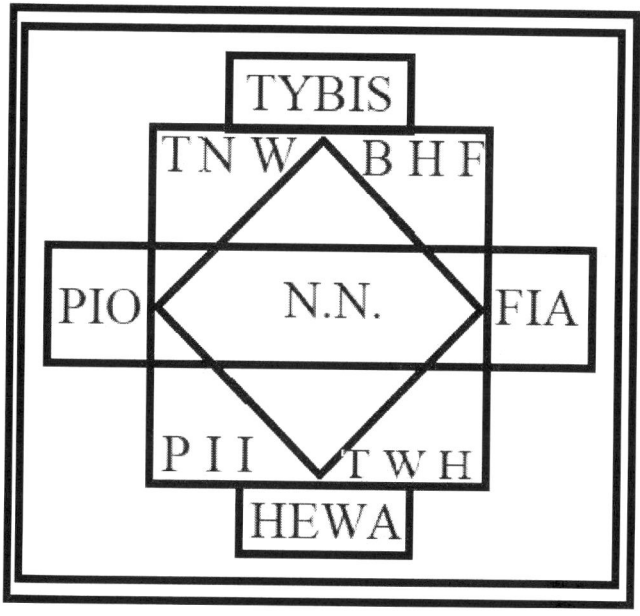

Obtain a small wooden box and line the bottom with virgin clay. Smooth the clay flat and even, and engrave the above seal, replacing N.N. with the target's name, directly onto the clay with an iron nail. Once a day, read the Psalm over the opened box and strike three matches at once. They must all burn on the first strike. Toss them into the box and shut the lid. Repeat this daily until the person does as you wish. When they have succumbed to your will, open the box and throw it and it's contents into running water.

TO PUNISH BETRAYAL

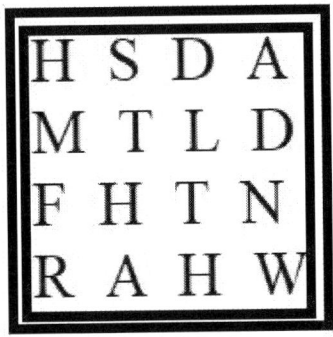

Mark the above seal on lead on a Saturday in the Hour of Saturn. Fumigate it with nine match heads and peppercorn. Pray the psalm nine times over the seal, and bury it where the person will walk over it.

TO KILL FISH

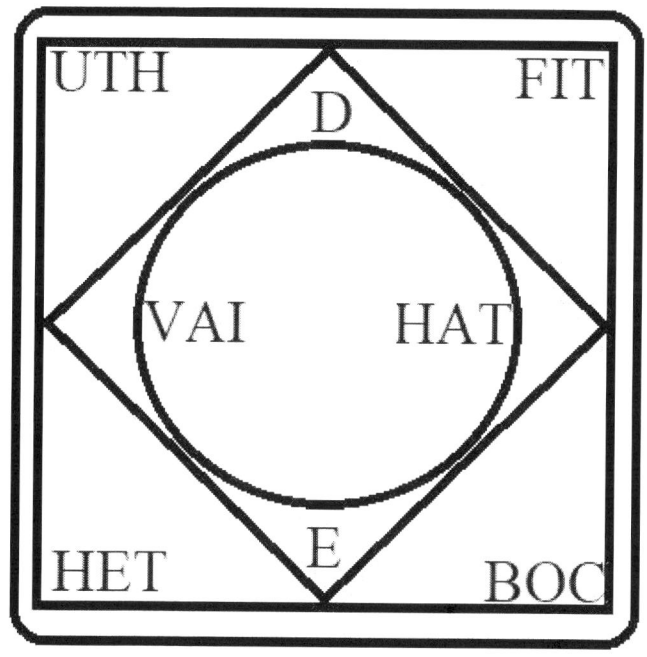

Mark the above seal on iron and fumigate it with powdered snake. Pray the psalm five times over the seal and cast it over your left shoulder into the body of water.

PSALM 106

TO CAUSE FLOODS

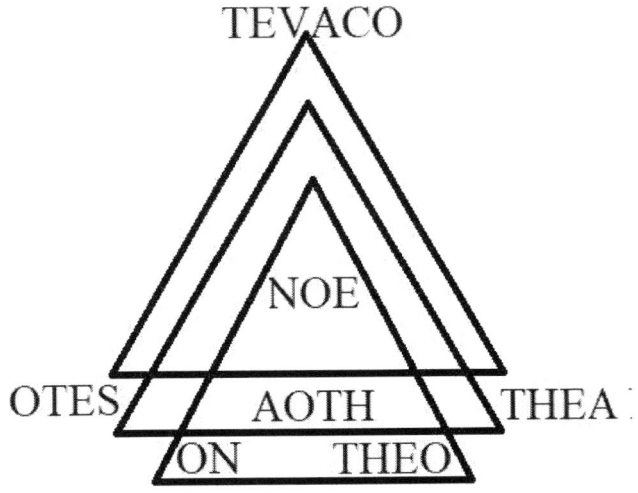

Mark the above seal on silver, engraving it with iron, and fumigating it with the skin of a freshwater fish, willow, and camphor. Pray the psalm three times over the seal and place it in a jar of water suspended from the east side of a tree.

TO PUNISH INFIDELITY WITH DISEASE

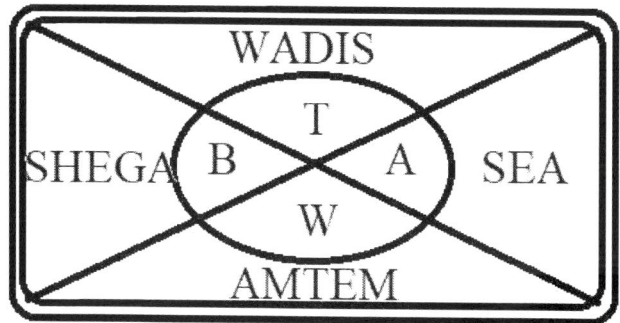

Mark the above seal in the blood of a pig directly upon the undergarments of the unfaithful one. Fumigate it with a mixture of patchouli, asafoetida, and myrtle. Pray the psalm 5 times - four to the cardinal directions; and the fifth time directly over the garment. Burn the garment to ashes and scatter the ashes on the western side of a hospital.

TO RELEASE THE IMPRISONED

Mark the above seal on clean parchment, writing the name of the person within the circle, and carry it to a Sunday Mass and when the Host is elevated, whisper the name of the imprisoned onto the seal. Take this seal home and fumigate it with frankincense and comfrey while praying the psalm three times over the seal. Afterwards, keep it in a bible over the psalm.

TO PROTECT A PRISONER

```
HECAL VOHE THECATO SOTEM
HECAL VOHE THECATO SOTEM
HECAL VOHE THECATO SOTEM
```

Write the above seal on clean parchment and on the back, write the full name and birthdate of the prisoner. On a Sunday at dawn, collect dirt from the east side of a church, and roll the seal around it. Fumigate the seal with angelica and place it in a small bottle. Pray the psalm three times into the bottle every day, and close it afterwards. Keep the bottle in a high and safe place, but not in the dark.

PSALM 107

FOR A HAPPY MARRIAGE

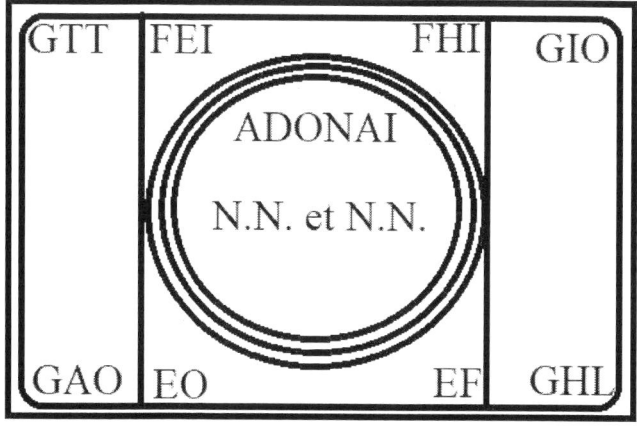

Inscribe the above seal on gold foil with a stylus composed of the 3rd left wing feather of a white goose, replacing N.N. et N.N. with your name and the name of your spouse. Fumigate it with orange and roll the seal into a small scroll, placing it within a small vial or locket. Pray the psalm seven times over the seal. Carry the seal close to your heart.

TO REMOVE BLOCKAGES AND DRAGGING SPIRITS

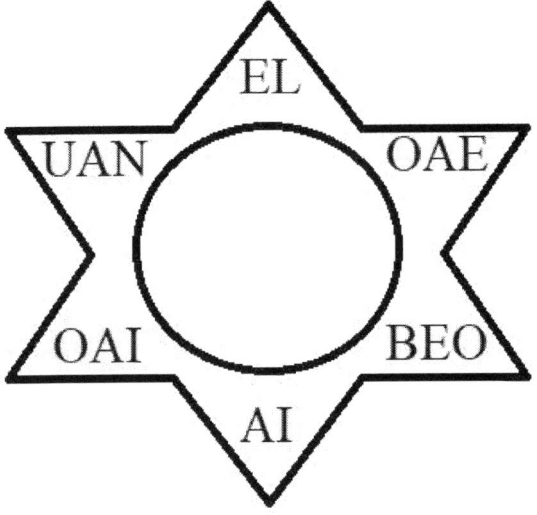

Make six of the above seals on clean parchment in orange ink, and within the circle mark it with one drop of your blood. On a Sunday in the hour of the Sun, pray the psalm six times, after each recitation burning one of the seals, and fumigating yourself with the smoke. Repeat this until each seal is consumed. The ashes are to be thrown out of your front door.

TO FIND A HOME
HELET BASYA TACIT VETHECOS

Write the above words on clean parchment during the elevation of the Host at Mass. Take the parchment and wrap it around a statue of St. Joseph with a green thread. Fumigate the statue in bergamot and coriander while praying the psalm three times. Place the image on a high place with a glass of water, which you will pour out on the ground every day while saying the Lord's prayer.

TO KEEP SOMEONE IN PRISON

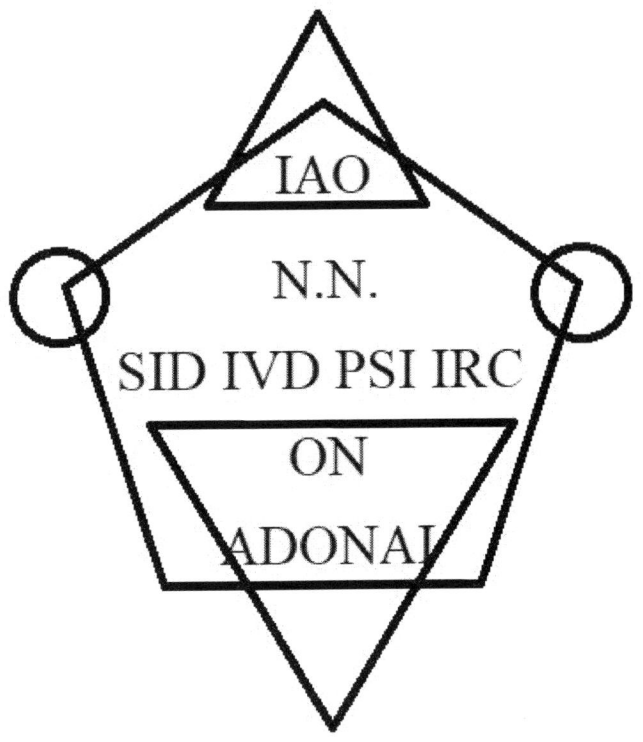

Mark the above seal on lead during the day and hour of Saturn, replacing N.N. with the name of the person. Fumigate it with sulfur and pray the psalm 9 times over the seal and bury it in the center of a dirt road.

TO CAUSE WASTING

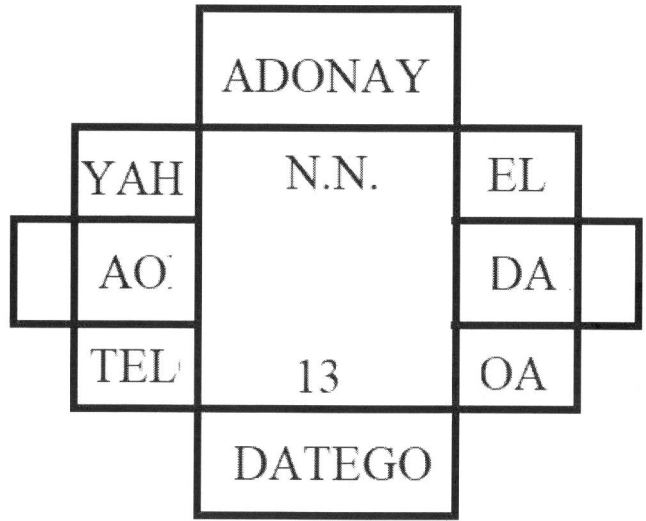

Mark the above seal on a piece of pig's skin in black ink during the hour of Mars on the day of Saturn and fumigate it with devil's snuff, replacing N.N. with the name of the victim. Pray the psalm three times over it, and bury it in the grave of a child that never cried.

TO RECEIVE HONORS

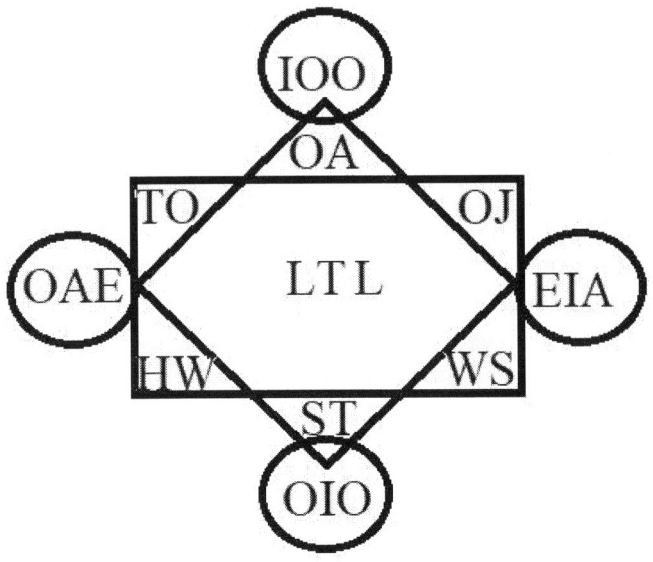

Mark the above seal on clean copper in the day of Jupiter in the hour of Venus and fumigate it with rose and clove. Pray the psalm over it 7 times and wear it near your heart. Fumigate it and repeat the prayers on Fridays when the moon grows only, to keep the charm active.

TO CALM A STORM

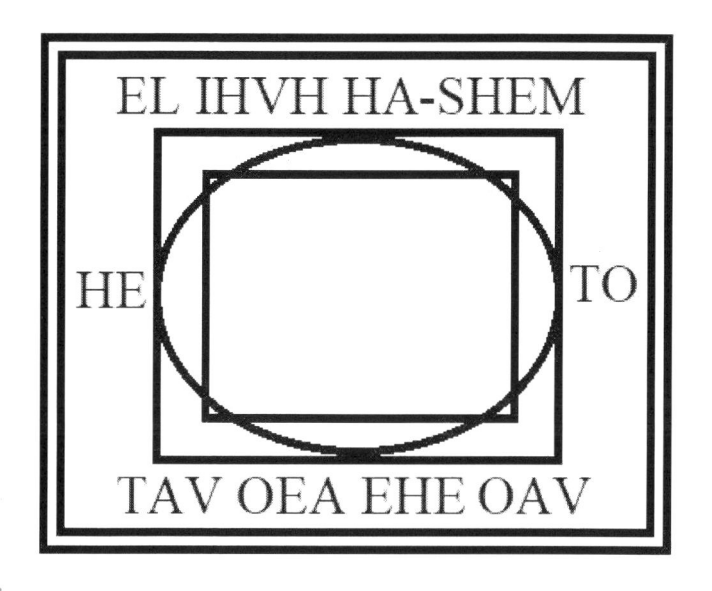

![Seal with text: EL IHVH HA-SHEM at top, HE on left, TO on right, TAV OEA EHE OAV at bottom]

Mark the above seal on silver during the day and hour of the Moon and fumigate it with camphor, while praying the psalm three times. When you wish to calm a storm, heat the talisman gently in the oven while praying the psalm.

TO SILENCE THE MOUTHS OF THE WICKED

```
        VI
       ARB
       TUSA
       REBAT
       UEOU
        TVS
    STM   I   ATV
```

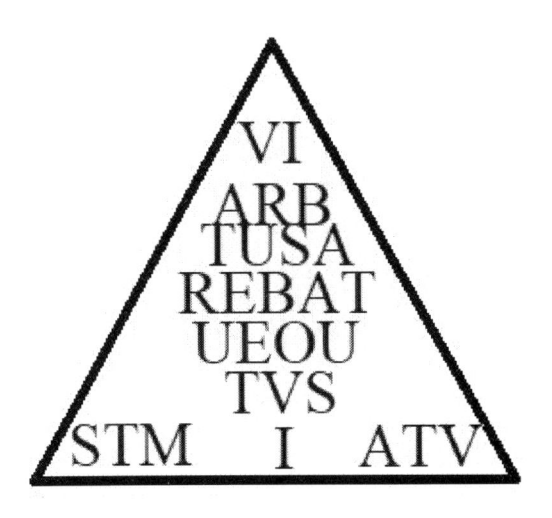

Mark the above seal on a piece of lead and stain the words with ochre. On the back of the seal, write the names of the perpetrators and bury the seal, names facing down, in the grave of a stillborn child on a Saturday during the hour of Saturn, praying the psalm three times over the seal.

PSALM 108

TO KEEP A PERSON LOYAL TO YOU

IAH EL

M	H	O	G
I	S	I	W
S	A	M	M
W	A	M	S

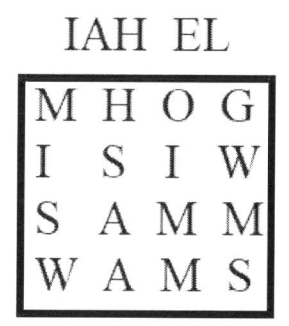

MIHE EL ISIV SAMA MUA MIS

Make the above seal on leather using your own blood as ink at sunrise on a Wednesday with the Moon increasing. Write the person's name on the back, and the divine names IAH EL above it, and the words MIHE EL ISIV SAMA MUA MIS below it. This is to me fumigated with frankincense and myrrh while praying the psalm three times. Keep the seal in your left pocket.. On Fridays at 3pm, pray 3 Our Fathers over the seal in honor of the Crucifixion, then read the divine names, the target's name and MIHE, etc. over the seal.

TO RECEIVE HELP FROM LOVED ONES

Mark the above seal on clean parchment during the day and hour of the Sun and fumigate it with calamus while praying the psalm 6 times over it. Bind the square to your right hand when asking for help.

TO CONQUER OPPOSITION

V EL V V G T V A H V T D O E

Write the above letters on a piece of iron in your own blood on a Tuesday during the hour of Mars. Fumigate it with peppermint while praying the psalm 5 times. Carry it with you in your left pocket.

PSALM 109

TO CAUSE A PERSON TO BE HATED

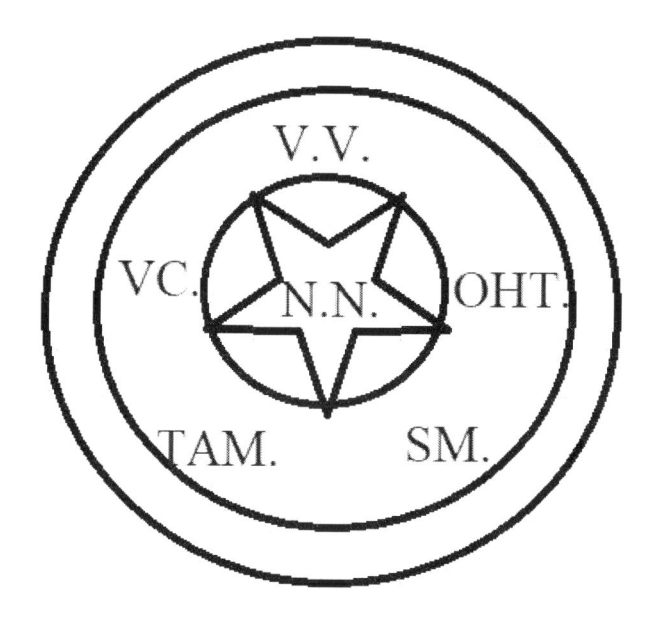

Mark the above seal on lead, using an iron nail, on a Saturday during the hour of Mars, replacing N.N. with the target's initials. On the back, write the target's name, and the name of their mother such as - John Doe son of Jane (maiden name)". Fumigate the seal with sulfur and peppercorn and pray the psalm nine times over it. Then take the seal, fold it over, and use the same iron nail from engraving it to nail the seal onto the western side of a thorn tree at sunset on a Tuesday.

TO DESTROY AN ENEMY

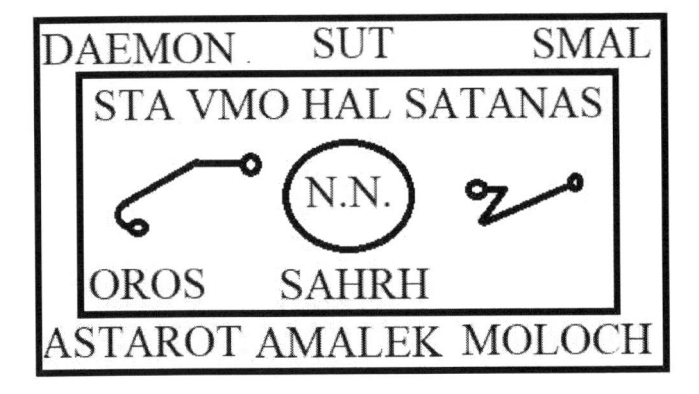

```
┌─────────────────────────────────────┐
│ DAEMON   SUT        SMAL            │
│ ┌─────────────────────────────────┐ │
│ │  STA VMO HAL SATANAS            │ │
│ │      ╭─○      ╭─○               │ │
│ │     (  N.N. )                   │ │
│ │      ╰○       ╰○                │ │
│ │  OROS    SAHRH                  │ │
│ └─────────────────────────────────┘ │
│  ASTAROT AMALEK MOLOCH              │
└─────────────────────────────────────┘
```

Mark the above seal on goatskin parchment or leather on a Saturday at the stroke of midnight, replacing N.N. with the name of your enemy; the whole being written in black ink, and the best pen for the operation would be a quill fashioned from a corvid feather. Place a small pile of sulfur on top of the individual's name, and tie the seal around it using a thread that has touched a corpse (easily done by taking a spool of thread to a funeral home for a visitation.) Dig a small hole in the grave of a unrepentant criminal and place the package, praying the psalm nine times into the hole before covering it. After the hole is covered, you are to smash a bottle of cooking vinegar over the tombstone.

TO CAUSE A JUDGE TO CONDEMN A PERSON

```
┌─────────────────────────────┐
│ V.H.S. B.I.L. H.B.C.        │
│ H.                     B.   │
│ S.         ╭─────╮     H.   │
│ S.        │ N.N. │     H.   │
│ H.         ╰─────╯          │
│                         B.  │
│ V.H.S. B.I.L. H.B.C.        │
└─────────────────────────────┘
```

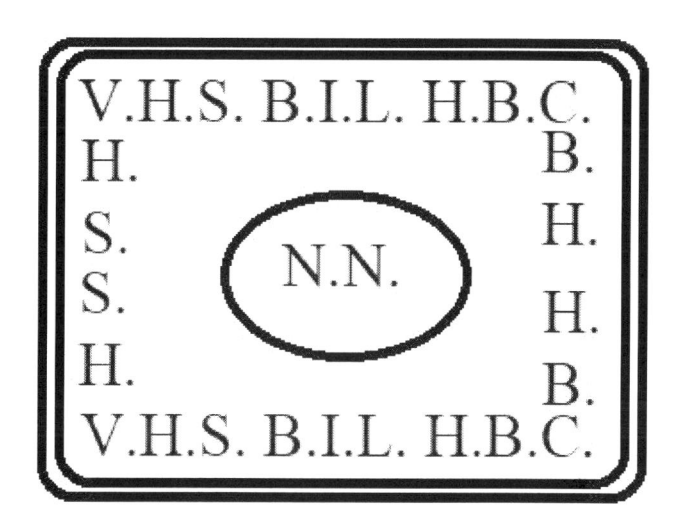

Write the above seal on lead during the day and hour of Saturn and fumigate it with myrrh, replacing N.N. with the name of the target. Pray the psalm nine times over the seal, and conceal it somewhere on the property of the court where the case will be tried.

TO CAUSE A PERSON TO LOSE THEIR POSITION OR OFFICE

Mark the above seal on clean parchment on a Tuesday during the hour of Saturn in iron gall ink, replacing N.N. with the name of the target. Fumigate this seal with a mixture of peppercorn, arrowroot, and sulfur while praying the psalm five times.. Wrap the seal around a sprig of mugwort, tying it still with a red string. Place the seal within the mouth of a fish and use three hooks to close the mouth. Bury the fish in a box of salt in a drainage ditch or creek bed on a Friday at sunset.

TO CAUSE AUDITS, FINANCIAL LEANS, AND DEBT

```
┌─────────────────────────────┐
│        EL ON LEX            │
│    ┌───────────────┐        │
│    │    L TE       │        │
│    │    N.N.       │        │
│    │    C A T H    │        │
│    └───────────────┘        │
│      TETRAX ELOHE           │
└─────────────────────────────┘
```

Strive to obtain a dollar, a receipt, or some financial paper of the individual, and on the day and hour of Saturn, the moon decreasing, write the above seal in black ink upon it, replacing N.N. with the name of the individual. Fumigate the seal nine times with myrrh and nine times with sulphur, reciting the psalm nine times over the seal. Burn the seal to ashes and seal it within a bottle which will then be cast over your left shoulder into a running river or the ocean at low tide.

PSALM 110

TO CONQUER ENEMIES

```
  STA
MRH VTI
 MTE TF
```

ADONAI ELOHIM

Mark the above seal on a small medallion of steel when the Angelus rings, and on the back write the divine names ADONAI ELOHIM. Fumigate the medallion with sandalwood and pray the psalm three times over it. The medallion must then be carried to three masses and held in the hands when the priest gives the benediction. It may then be worn as an amulet.

TO REMOVE MISFORTUNE

```
H S D O
T B I T
W T S H
L U T H
```

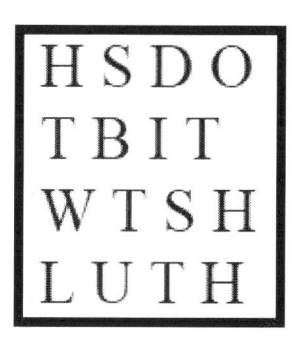

Mark the above square on the bottom of a new white bowl or cup with the juice of a pomegranate. Fill the vessel with spring water and pray the psalm nine times over it. Afterwhich, take three sips of the liquid, then pour the rest over your head.

PSALM 111

TO NEVER BE WITHOUT

HAVA NEAA MEL VEN OSV

Pray the psalm seven times over a piece of new chalk, and write the above words over your door.

PSALM 112

TO MAKE A MAN VIRILE

H S S B M V E
EL ON ELOHA AB TETRA
EHEIEH ASHER EHEIEH

Write the above words on clean goatskin parchment in pure ink and pray the psalm five times over it, during the day and hour of Mars. Fumigate it with peppermint and pray the psalms 5 times again, daily for five days. Afterwhich, burn the seal to ashes and rub the ashes on your member.

FOR WEALTH

```
V A R S B H H
     EL
   ADONAI
HEH         BET
```

Obtain a new wooden box and write the above seal on all sides, inside and out, in gold ink. Within the box place a lock of your hair, a piece of silver, a piece of gold, and three drops of your own blood. Fumigate the box with frankincense while praying the psalm six times at sunrise on a Sunday. Keep the box in a high clean place.

TO OBTAIN A LOAN

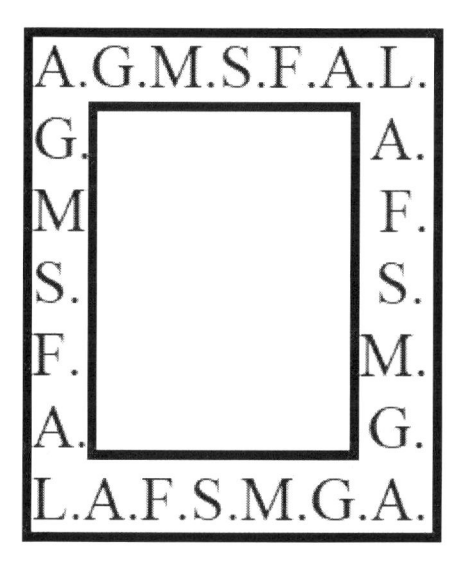

```
A.G.M.S.F.A.L.
G.           A.
M.           F.
S.           S.
F.           M.
A.           G.
L.A.F.S.M.G.A.
```

On a Sunday or a Thursday, moon increasing, write the above square on the surface of a compact mirror in green ink during the hour of Venus. Fumigate it with rose and coriander while praying the psalm seven times over it. Catch the reflection of the person in the compact and close it. Carry this with you when you see a loan from them, praying the psalm over it and tapping it seven times.

PSALM 113

TO REVERSE FINANCIAL MISFORTUNE

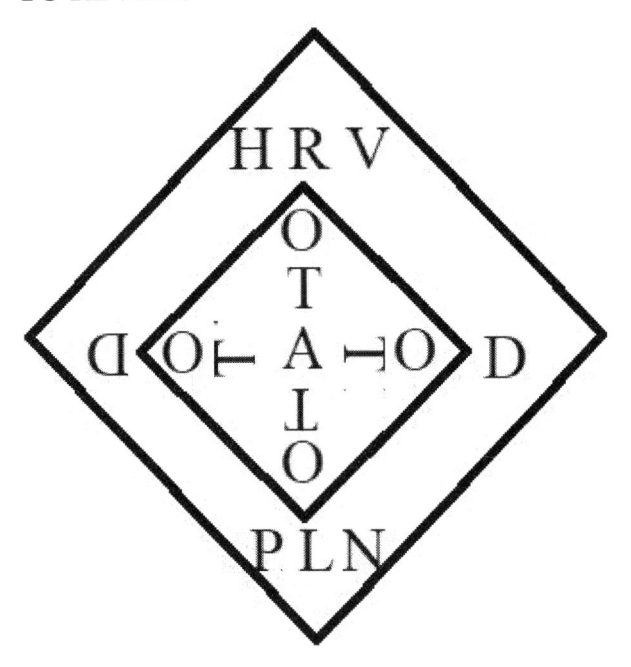

Mark the above seal on copper during the day and hour of Venus and fumigate it with rose, marigold, and chamomile, while praying the psalm 7 times. Carry the seal in your wallet.

FOR A WOMAN TO CONCEIVE

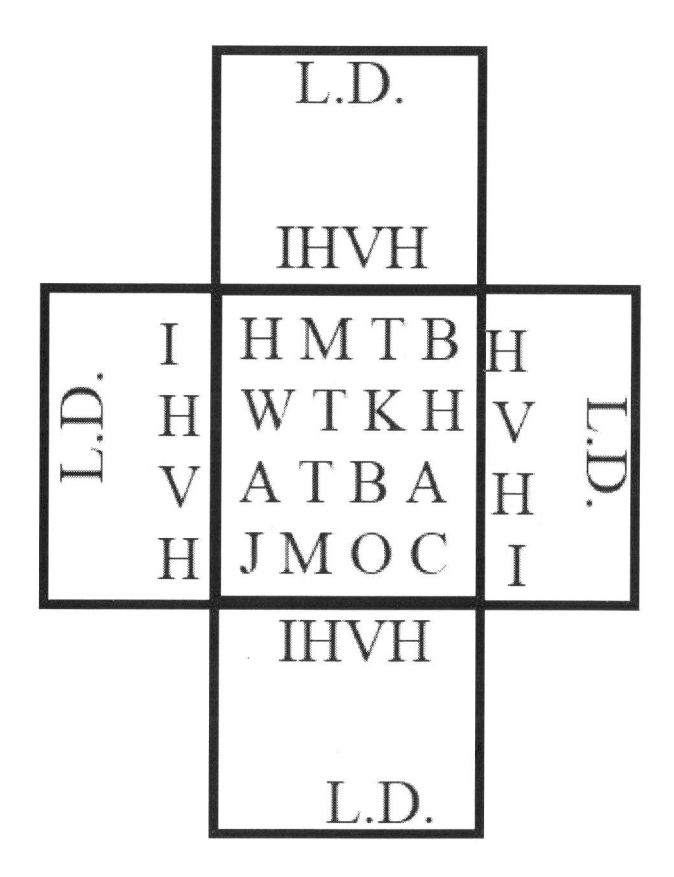

```
                    L.D.

                    IHVH

        I      HMTB    H
   L    H      WTKH    V    L
   .    V      ATBA    H    .
   D    H      JMOC    I    D
   .                        .

                    IHVH

                    L.D.
```

Obtain holy water from a church on a Sunday and soak a new piece of white cloth in it, then hang it up on a fruit bearing tree to dry. After it has dried, write the above seal on the cloth in blue ink and fumigate it with copal to which you have added three strands of your hair and nine drops of your blood. Pray the psalm seven times over the seal, and lay it across your womb every day, while reciting the psalm.

PSALM 114

TO TURN BACK FLOOD WATERS

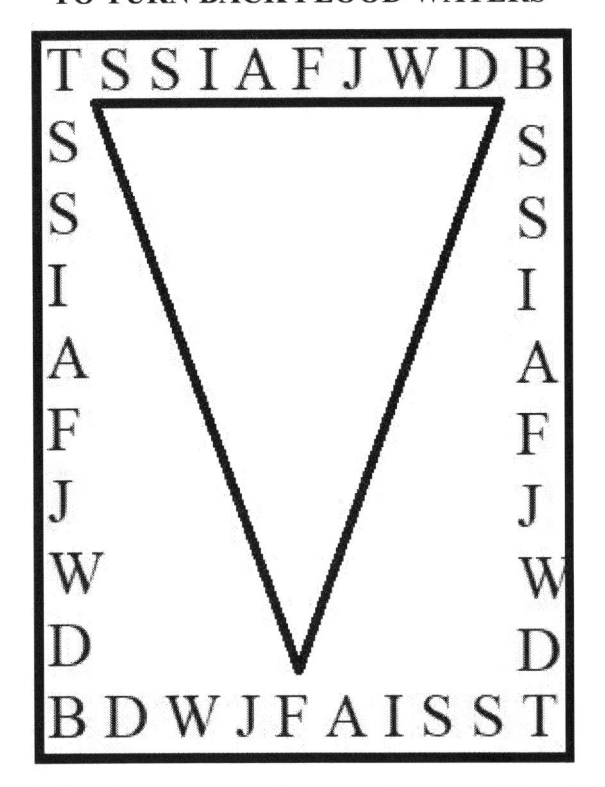

```
T S S I A F J W D B
S                 S
S                 S
I                 I
A                 A
F                 F
J                 J
W                 W
D                 D
B D W J F A I S S T
```

Mark the above sea on clean parchment with red ink and pray the psalm nine times over it, fumigating it with myrrh. Cast the seal over your left shoulder into the waters.

PROTECTION FROM EVIL SPIRITS

```
        EL
   AE  ATH  OC
      ADONAI
   SOE      ROH
        TO
```

Mark the above seal on gold foil on the day and hour of the Sun and and fumigate it with sandalwood. Carry it in a glass vial around your neck on a gold chain.

PSALM 115

TO BIND SOMEONE'S MOUTH

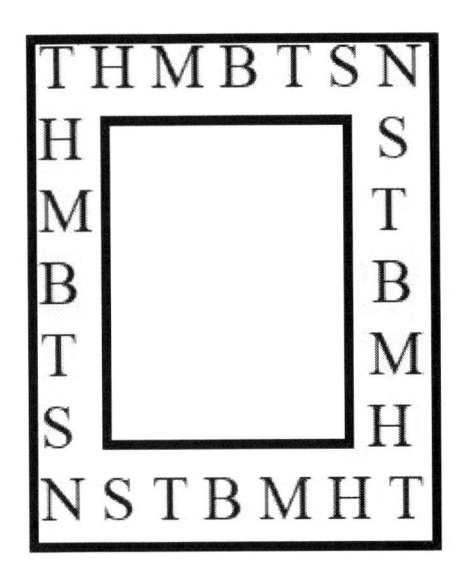

```
T H M B T S N
H           S
M           T
B           B
T           M
S           H
N S T B M H T
```

Mark the above seal on lead during the day and hour of Saturn, writing the name of the person within the blank square. Fumigate it with myrrh and pray the psalm 9 times over it and bury it in the grave of a child that never cried.

TO BIND SOMEONE'S EYES

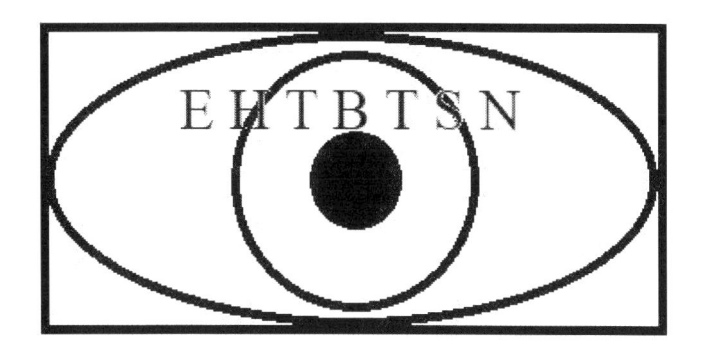

Mark the above seal on lead during the day and hour of Saturn and fumigate it with sulfur while praying the psalm 9 times over it. Drive a nail through the eye on the seal, and bury it where the person will walk over it.

TO BIND SOMEONE'S EARS

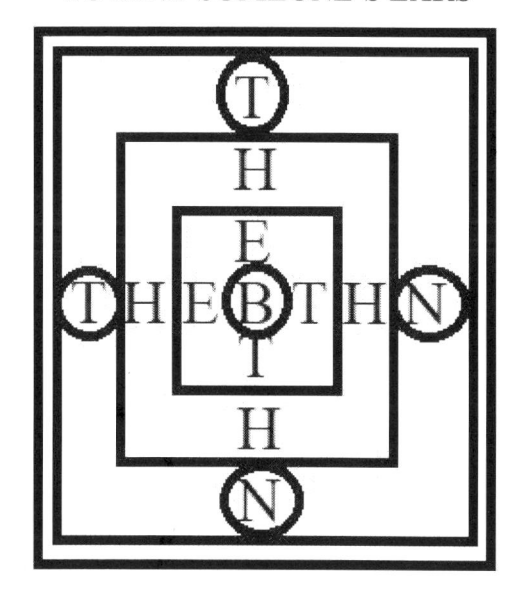

Mark the above seal on lead during the day and hour of Saturn and fumigate it with sulfur while praying the psalm nine times over it. On the back, write the name of the person and hide the seal in a bell tower.

PSALM 116

AGAINST ANXIETY

R V T R O M S F ADONAI H D B VV T

Write the above characters upon clean parchment during the day and hour of the Sun and fumigate with frankincense while praying the psalm six times. Burn the seal to ash, mix the ash with rain water, and drink the liquid.

AGAINST DEPRESSION

```
OOA EY UOE IE OA AY EOA
EL TETRAGRAMMATON ELOHIM
```

Mark the above seal on sheepskin parchment during the day and hour of the Sun and fumigate it with frankincense while praying the psalm 6 times. Burn the seal to ashes and rub the ash into your scalp.

PSALM 117

FOR ASSISTANCE

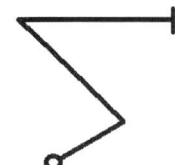

> O praise the Lord, all ye nations: praise him, all ye people.
> For his merciful kindness is great toward us: and the truth of the Lord endureth for ever. Praise ye the Lord.

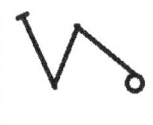

Write the above seal on a piece of clean white linen, which is the verse of the psalm coupled with the signatures on either side. Set an olive oil lamp to burn over the cloth on a white plate and pray the psalm 33 times. After this, fold the cloth and place it under your pillow.

PSALM 118

FOR PROTECTION IN BATTLE

ADONAI IOYIEIIOEAAAAOUOE ADONAI

Carry the above words, written on clean parchment during the consecration of an Easter Mass, and consecrated by the recitation of the psalm five times, and you will be safe from men in battle.

TO ASSIST THE GRAVELY ILL

```
┌─────────────────────────────────┐
│           ADONAI                │
│      ┌─────────────┐            │
│  ╱─╲ │   I S N D   │  ╱─╲       │
│ │   ││   BL A D    │ │   │      │
│  ╲─╱ │   TWO A     │  ╲─╱       │
│      └─────────────┘            │
│   IAOIEUIEAEAEEOOEO             │
└─────────────────────────────────┘
```

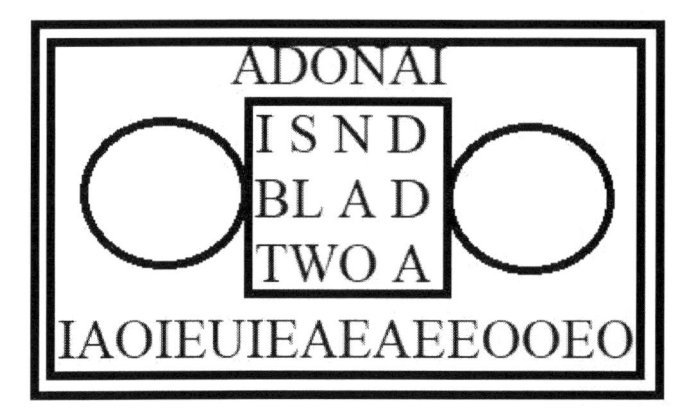

Mark the above seal on gold foil with the feather of a dove, writing the name of the individual in the left circle, and their birthdate in the other. Fumigate the seal with frankincense and myrrh and pray the psalm 7 times over it in honor of the 7 spirits that attend the throne of the Most High. Roll the seal around the dove feather, and place it under their pillow.

TO OPEN ROADS

```
          O
         EE
       ADONAI
      ┌─────────┐
      │ O T M T │
   OE │ G O R I │ IO
   EIO│ W G I T │ OE
   AEA│ A I W P │ AIII
   EI IE└───────┘EOU
```

Mark the above seal on tin during the day and hour of Jupiter and fumigate it with clove while praying the psalm 4 times over it. Wear the seal around your neck on a blue cord.

FOR FINANCIAL HELP

```
┌─────────────────────────────┐
│      EEE  /AEO\  EEO        │
│     ADONAI ELOHIM           │
│         OOEI                │
│         OOO                 │
│      EEE SNP EEE            │
└─────────────────────────────┘
```

Mark the above seal on clean parchment during the day of Mercury in the hour of the Sun, the moon increasing, and burn 3 white candles on top of it, in honor of the Most Holy Trinity, while praying the psalm three times for the same.

PSALM 119

TO MAKE A PERSON CONFESS

```
        AE
        /\
    UE /Y \ AE
      /----\
     / I  I \
    /--------\
   OU\  E  /AE
      \   /
       \ /
       OY
```

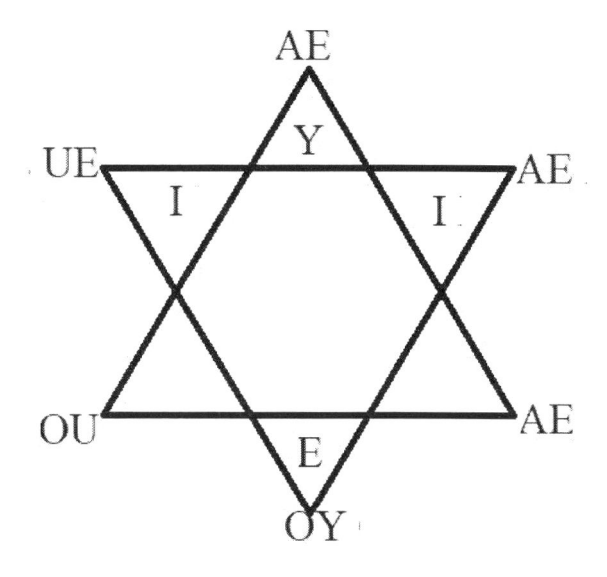

Write the above seal on clean parchment with a hen's feather in black ink. Within the empty triangles, write to the left the person's name, and to the right their birthdate. Within the center, write the question. At the stroke of midnight for nine nights, light a white candle on the seal and pray the psalm, before snuffing it out.

FOR GUIDANCE

```
┌─────────────────────┐
│ AIH  ╱╲  OMS        │
│    ╱    ╲           │
│   ╱      ╲          │
│  ╱  DOM   ╲         │
│   ╲      ╱          │
│    ╲    ╱           │
│ ALN  ╲╱  ITW        │
└─────────────────────┘
```

Mark the above seal in ink on a white plate and set a cotton wick and olive oil to burn upon it while praying the psalm six times and meditating on your question.

AGAINST OPPRESSION FROM MEN

DEME F.T.O OMA SIIE THECE

Carry the above seal in your left shoe, written on clean parchment and fumigated with copal and frankincense during the day and hour of Mercury, while praying the psalm 8 times.

PSALM 120

TO BE DELIVERED FROM LIES AND LIARS

```
        EIEYOU
ADONAI    ADONAI

OYIIAOAEEIUOUE
          EIEYOU
ADONAI    ADONAI
```

Mark the above seal on lead during the day and hour of Saturn. Fumigate the seal with myrrh and pray the psalm nine times over it. Lay the seal at the foot of a crucifix in a cemetery.

PSALM 121

TO MAINTAIN YOUR POSITION

```
         EIOUEYOOOEOE
    ┌────────────────────┐
    │        ╱NOS╲        │
    │      ╱HEVIOT╲      │
    │      ╲ OTOB ╱      │
    │FETHPETHEV╲╱VEHETHATUE│
    └────────────────────┘
          EAEEEEEIO
```

Write the above seal on a smooth river rock in white ink at sunrise on a Saturday and pray the psalm 9 times over the rock, while facing the sun, and fumigating it with myrrh. Keep the stone in your home or your office, whichever the case may be.

PSALM 122

Mark the above seal on white linen with red ink on a Sunday at dawn and fumigate it with frankincense while praying the psalm three times in honor of the trinity. Hang it up as a flag within your home for protection and prosperity.

PSALM 123

TO HOLD DOMINION

```
              AO
       OE    /AO\    EO
            /    \
           /  U   \
      AE  /── AA ──\  OE
   EI AE /╲ ┌────┐ ╱\ EO AE
         / OE│ EL │AE \
         \  └────┘   /
          \ EY UI UO/
         /EE\      /EE\
        /OU  \ADONAI\ OE\
```

IE OO UE EA IU IE UO EAAA

Mark the above seal in tin on a Thursday during the hour of Jupiter and fumigate it clove while praying the psalm 16 times over it. Carry the seal tied to your right arm.

PSALM 124

TO BE SAFE FROM THE ATTACKS OF WILD ANIMALS

```
┌─────────────────────────┐
│ GUA      TT       BBT   │
│      ┌─────────┐        │
│      │ ADONAI  │        │
│      └─────────┘        │
│ APT              WHN    │
└─────────────────────────┘
```

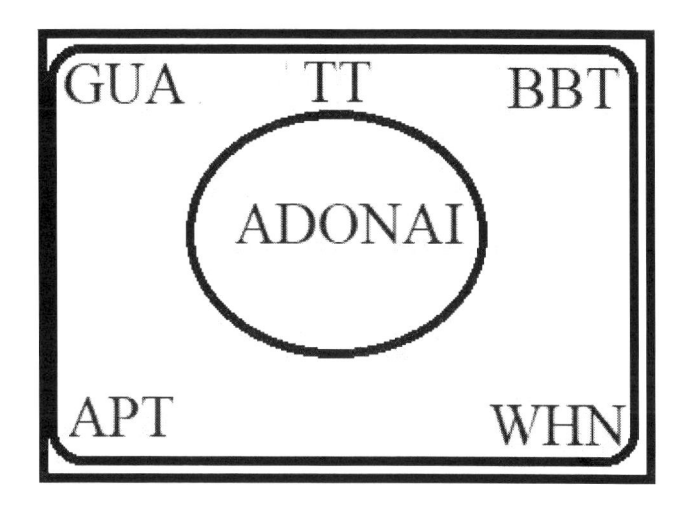

Write the above seal in iron gall ink on goatskin parchment on a Tuesday during the hour of Mars. Fumigate it with peppermint while praying the psalm five times over it. Carry it in your left sock.

TO ESCAPE CAPTURE

```
        AAI
   OE         AE
      EL ABBA
      EAEOEIE
   OU         OU
        OUO
```

Mark the above seal in aluminum with a stolen nail on the day and hour of Mercury. Fumigate it with lavender and and pray the psalm 8 times. Wear the seal around your ankle.

PSALM 125

FOR PROTECTION

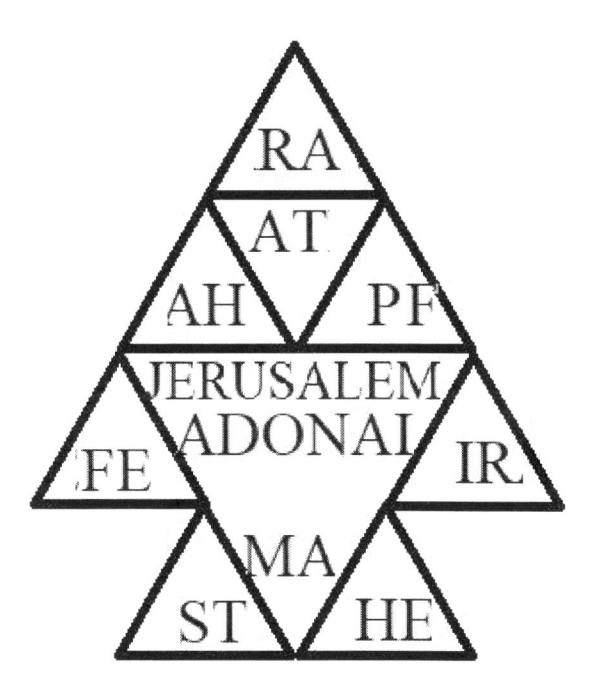

Mark the above seal on an arrowhead of flint or iron in red ink on a Sunday during the hour of mars. Fumigate it with frankincense and pray the psalm 6 times over the seal. Carry it in a red pouch near your heart.

TO BE PROTECTED FROM ROBBERS

```
┌─────────────────────┬─────────────────────┐
│                  O  │                     │
│                  E  │                     │
│                  I  │                     │
│  For the rod of  E  │  the wicked shall   │
│                  O  │                     │
│                  A  │                     │
│                  O  │                     │
│                  E  │                     │
├─────OEOOEIEAOE──────┼──UOEOOEIEOU─────────┤
│                  U  │                     │
│                  O  │                     │
│                  E  │                     │
│  not rest upon the  O  lot of the righteous│
│                  O  │                     │
│                  E  │                     │
│                  I  │                     │
│                  E  │                     │
└─────────────────────┴─────────────────────┘
```

Mark the above seal on lead during the hour of Saturn on Wednesday and fumigate it with myrrh while praying the psalm 8 times. Hang it above your door or carry it wrapped in black cloth in a safe container in your wallet.

PSALM 126

TO REVERSE MISFORTUNE

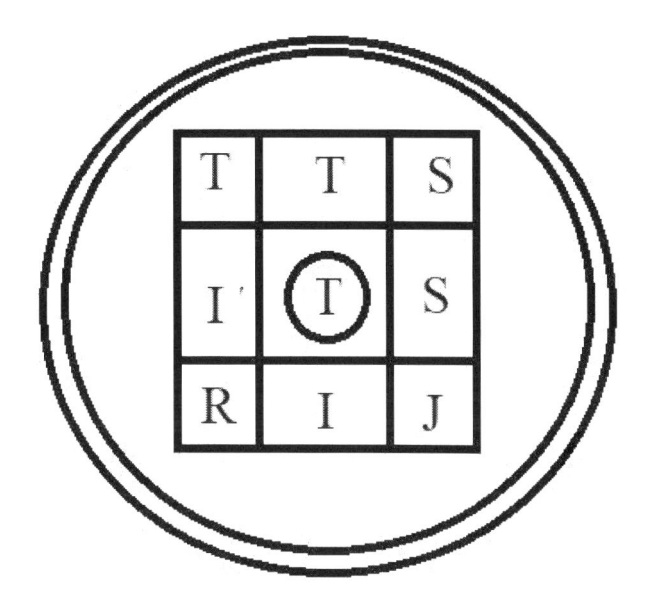

Take earthenware clay and pray the psalm three times over it, and mix your own tears into the clay. Form a flat disk in the clay and write the seal upon it. When the clay has dried, fumigate it with frankincense and myrrh, praying the psalms again, then dissolve the seal in your bathwater, again praying the psalms. Bathe in the water.

PSALM 127

TO BECOME PREGNANT

OIEAEAEIAEOE
NET
IRE
OHOS
ADONAY

OIEAEAEIAEOE

Mark the above seal on copper during a full moon in the hour of Venus, preferably on a Friday. Fumigate the seal with rose and pray the psalm over it 7 times. Place the seal under your mattress.

PSALM 128

FOR EMPLOYMENT

```
┌─────────────────────────────────┐
│   ┌─────────────────┐           │
│   │      BET        │           │
│   │ L           T   │           │
│HAO│ O    E      A   │OTAT       │
│   │ E           H   │           │
│   │      NIL        │           │
│   └─────────────────┘           │
└─────────────────────────────────┘
```

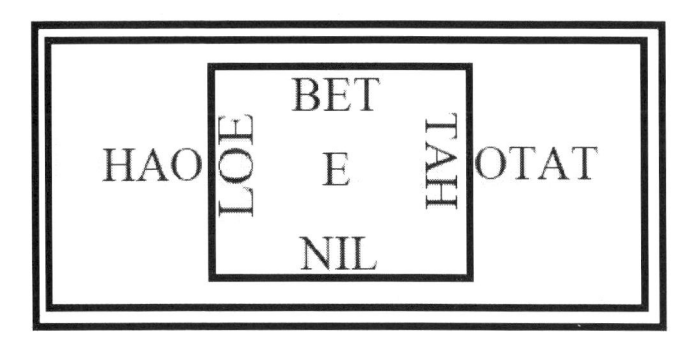

Write the above seal on the top of both of your feet in orange ink. Pray the psalm four times over your left foot, and four times over your right, before going to search for a job.

FOR GRANDCHILDREN

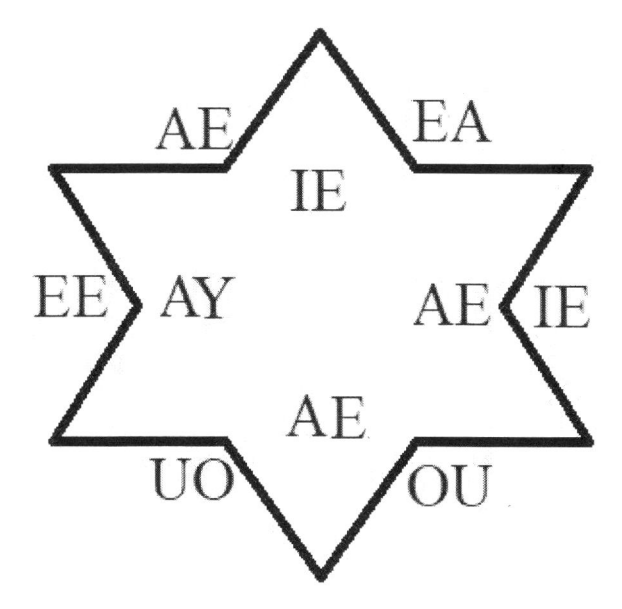

```
            AE     EA
               IE
        EE  AY      AE  IE
               AE
            UO     OU
```

Mark the above seal on a green plate in white ink at sunrise on a Friday and burn an olive oil lamp on top of it, while praying the psalm 7 times.

PSALM 129

TO DESTROY PLOTS AGAINST YOU

```
┌─────────────────────┐
│ TUTO  ╱╲    IAO     │
│      ╱  ╲           │
│     ╱    ╲          │
│    ╱ ADONAI╲        │
│     ╲    ╱          │
│      ╲  ╱           │
│ IREA  ╲╱    OEI     │
└─────────────────────┘
```

Write the above seal in red ink on a piece of broken pottery. Fumigate it with peppercorn, and pray the psalm five times over it. Head the seal in the oven slowly for five hours, then toss it in cold water.

TO CAUSE CONFUSION IN ENEMIES

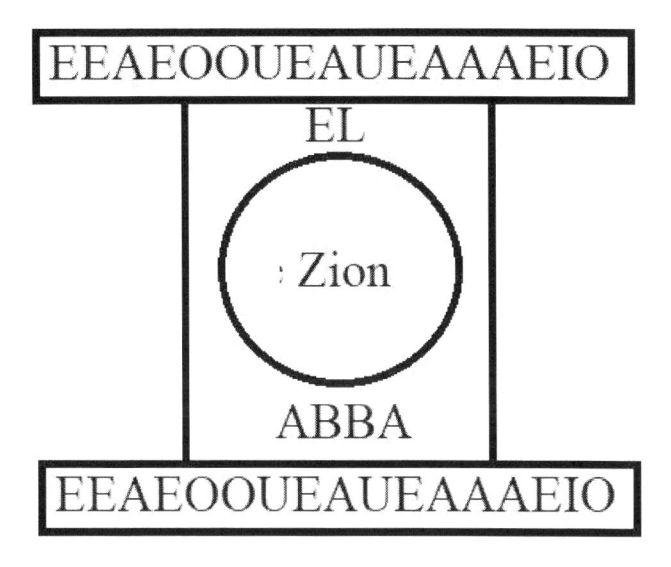

```
┌─────────────────────────────┐
│ EEAEOOUEAUEAAAEIO           │
├─────────────────────────────┤
            EL
         ╭───────╮
         │ :Zion │
         ╰───────╯
           ABBA
┌─────────────────────────────┐
│ EEAEOOUEAUEAAAEIO           │
└─────────────────────────────┘
```

Mark the above seal on goatskin parchment at noon on a Wednesday in black ink. Fumigate the seal with red pepper and copal; while praying the psalm 8 times over it. Hang the seal from a cord on the west side of a willow tree.

PSALM 130

TO SUMMON THE DEAD

Out of the depths have I cried unto thee, O Lord.

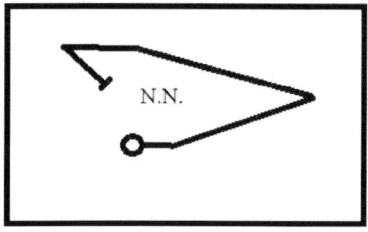

[Seal: N.N.]

I wait for the Lord, my soul doth wait, and in his word do I hope.

Write the above seal on clean parchment on the day of the week and during the time the person died, replacing N.N. with their name. On the back of the seal, write the verses of the psalm. Fumigate the seal with myrrh and pray the psalm 9 times. Leave the seal on your altar and the dead person will begin to contact you.

PSALM 131

TO HUMBLE THE ARROGANT

```
┌─────────────────────────────────┐
│  Y EAIO AUOIE EEOY EIEO         │
│                                 │
│         ADONAI                  │
│                                 │
│          N.N.                   │
│                                 │
│  EEIEEIEA AEOIIOO IOE           │
└─────────────────────────────────┘
```

Mark the above seal on a clay pot in black ink, replacing N.N. with the name of the person. Fill this pot with spring water and seven yellow flowers. Place on either side of the pot a white candle and pray the psalm 8 times over it. Allow the candles to burn out, and pour the water from the pot where the person will walk over it. The pot itself should be buried upside down on the western side of an oak tree.

PSALM 132

TO DEPRIVE A PERSON OF SLEEP

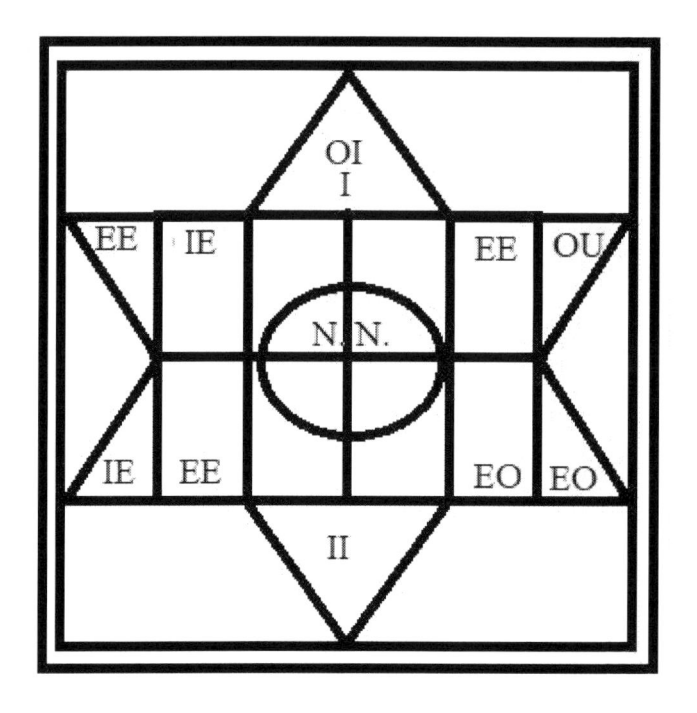

Write the above seal on the inside of a brass bell on a Wednesday during the hour of the Moon. Fumigate it with lavender and pray the psalm over the bell 8 times. Afterwards, when you believe the person to be asleep, ring the bell, and no matter where they are they will wake up.

TO MAKE A PERSON BEG FORGIVENESS

```
VV. VV. GIH. TVV.VV.. VV.A.H.F.
            N.N.
VV. VV. GIH. TVV.VV.. VV.A.H.F.
```

Write the above seal on a copper plate on the day of Venus in the hour of the Moon, replacing N.N. with the name of the person. Fumigate it with rose and lavender, and pray the psalm 7 times over it. Wear the seal under the sole of your left shoe.

TO BRING SHAME UPON YOUR ENEMIES

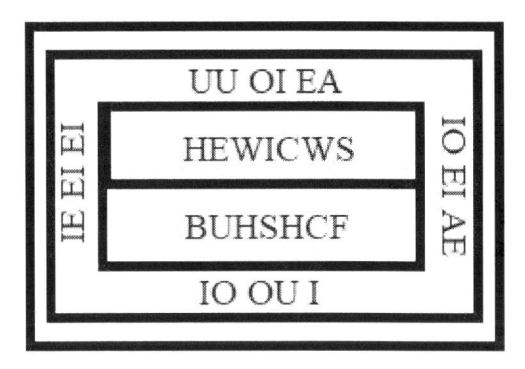

```
        UU OI EA
IE EI EI  HEWICWS  IO EI AE
          BUHSHCF
         IO OU I
```

Mark the above seal on tin on the day of Jupiter in the hour of Mars and fumigate it with clove and peppermint. Pray the psalm 4 times over the seal, and carry it in your left pocket when in the presence of your enemies.

PSALM 133

TO BRING PEACE BETWEEN PEOPLE

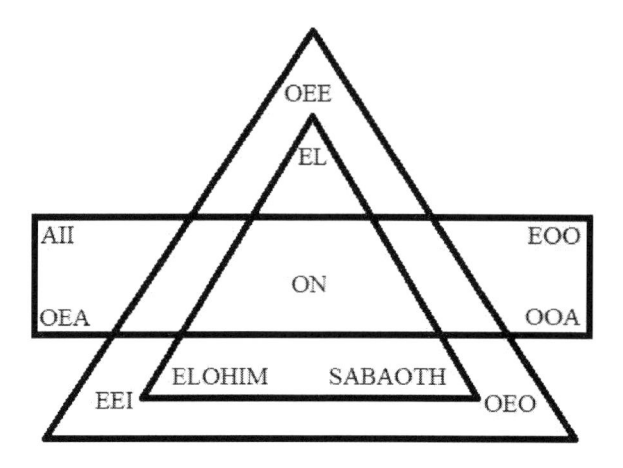

```
              OEE
              EL
    AII                  EOO
              ON
    OEA                  OOA
         ELOHIM  SABAOTH
     EEI                 OEO
```

Mark the above seal on copper during the day and hour of Venus and fumigate it with rose while praying the psalm 7 times. Take a piece of white cloth and on it write the names of the people in blue, and wrap this cloth around the seal. Keep the seal in a bible, on the page containing the psalm.

PSALM 134

TO PROTECT A HOME FROM DANGERS BY NIGHT

☧ Behold, bless ye the Lord, all ye servants of the Lord, which by night stand in the house of the Lord.
Lift up your hands in the sanctuary, and bless the Lord.
The Lord that made heaven and earth bless thee out of Zion. ☧

Write the seal on a clean piece of parchment, fumigating it with frankincense and myrrh on a holy day, and hang it over your door.

PSALM 135

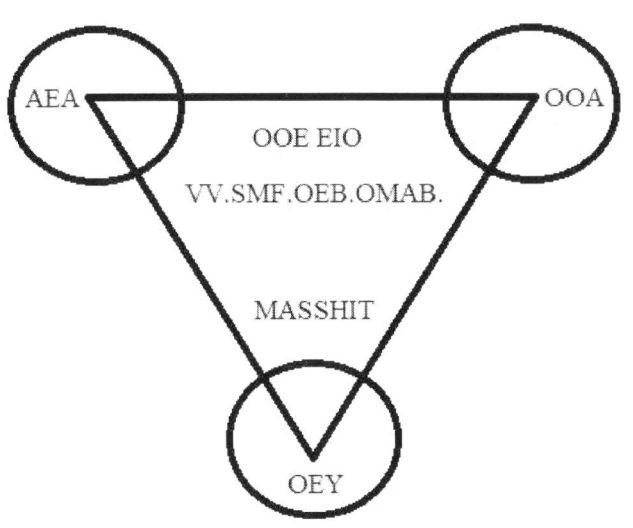

TO KILL THE FIRSTBORN

```
        AEA ─────────── OOA
           OOE EIO
         VV.SMF.OEB.OMAB.
            MASSHIT
             OEY
```

Mark the above seal on lead, during a solar eclipse; and pray the psalm nine times over it, fumigating it with sulfur. Wherever the seal is buried, the firstborn of man and beast will die.

PSALM 136

FOR WISDOM

```
┌─────────────────────────────┐
│  TIA YOAHE AVOS EDOV        │
│        ┌─────────┐          │
│   E    │    ◯    │   J      │
│   L    │         │   A      │
│   O    │         │   H      │
│   H    │         │   V      │
│   I    │         │   A      │
│   M    │         │   H      │
│        └─────────┘          │
│  TIA YOAHE AVOS EDOV        │
└─────────────────────────────┘
```

Mark the above seal on silver on a Monday during the hour of the Moon, preferably when it is full. Fumigate the seal with camphor and pray the psalm 13 times over it. Place it under your pillow.

TO SMITE POLITICIANS

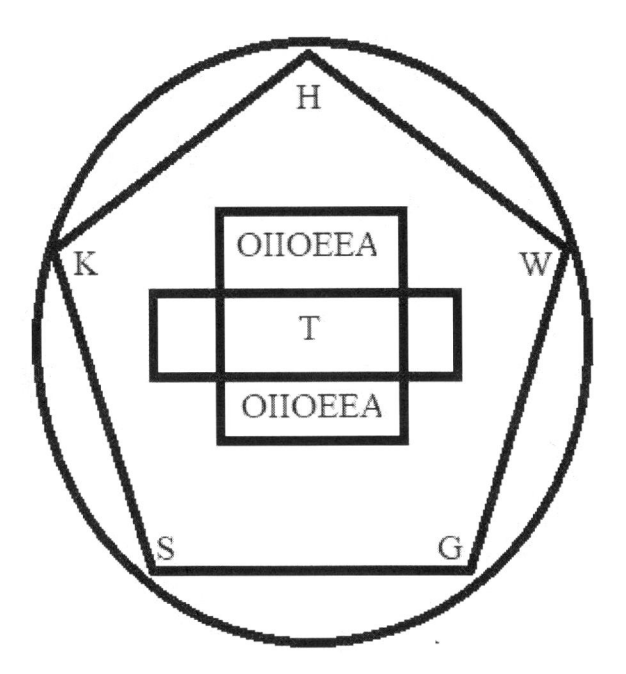

Mark the above seal on iron during the day and hour of Mars, in red ink. On the back, write the name of the politician and build a fire of martial woods, preferably five. Head the seal in the fire while praying the psalm five times and casting peppercorns into the fire.

PSALM 137

TO MAKE A PERSON GRIEVE FOR YOU

Mark the above seal on copper on Friday during the hour of Venus, replacing N.N. with the person's name, and fumigate it with rose and myrtle. Pray the psalm 7 times over it, and wear it from a green cord around your waist.

PSALM 138

TO MAKE A PERSON WORSHIP YOU

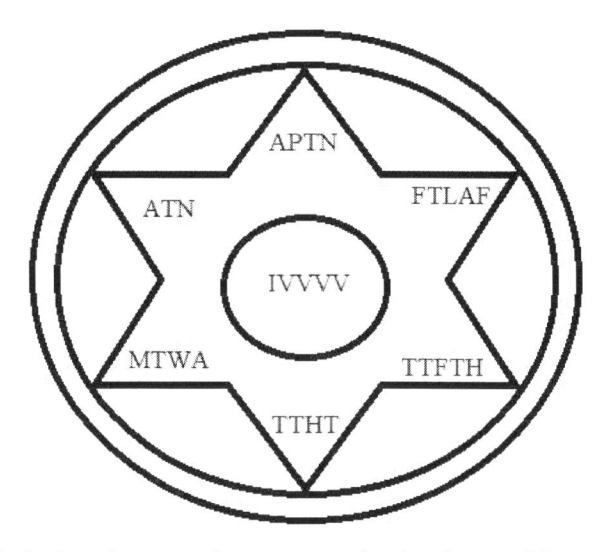

Mark the above seal on copper in the day and hour of Venus, with the Moon in Saturn and fumigate it with rose, while praying the psalm seven times. On the back, in green ink, write the name of the person you wish to dominate. Every Friday, pray the psalm seven times over the seal and fumigate it anew.

TO REVERSE HARM

> Though I walk in the midst of trouble, thou wilt revive me: thou shalt stretch forth thine hand against the wrath of mine enemies, and thy right hand shall save me.

Carry the above verse within two squares on a piece of virgin calfskin written with a white goose feather in black ink. Fumigate it with frankincense and myrrh on a Sunday at dawn.

PSALM 139

TO KNOW WHAT A PERSON SAYS ABOUT YOU

```
┌─────────┐
│ F T I N │
│ A W I M │
│ T B L A │
│ T K I A │
└─────────┘
```

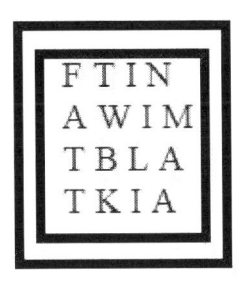

Write the above seal in grey ink on toadskin (cane toad leather is available online) during the day and hour of Mercury. Fumigate it with lavender and pray the psalm 8 times. When you wish to use it, let it come in contact with the person or some part of them, then pray the psalm and fumigate it again.

TO KNOW A PERSON'S WHEREABOUTS

```
        EEE
    AEE      OIE
       YII

   VV. S.I.G.F.T.S
        IE
   O.W.S.I.F.F.T.P.
        AI
    OO       OY
```

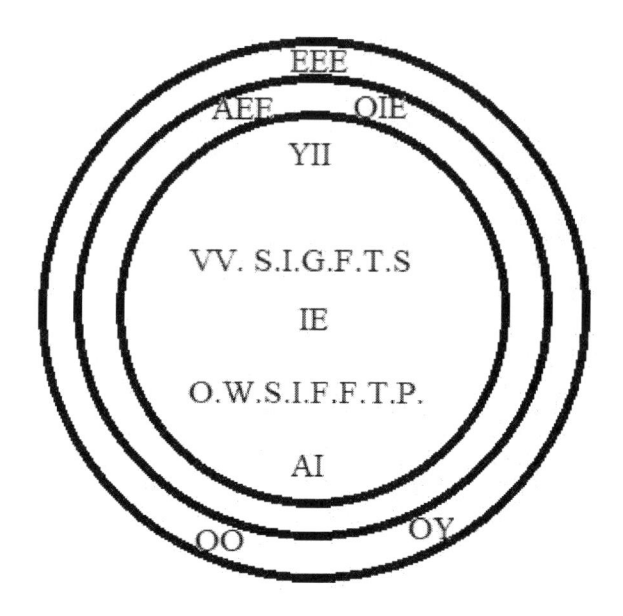

Mark the above seal on aluminum in the day and hour of Mercury, and fumigate it with lavender 8 times, reciting the psalm for each fumigation. On the back, engrave the name of the person you seek, and carry the seal with you.

PSALM 140

FOR PROTECTION FROM ENEMIES AND TROUBLESOME SITUATIONS

Mark the above seal on clean parchment, and write the psalm on the back. Pray the psalm five times over the seal and fumigate it with frankincense and peppermint. Carry the seal near your heart.

PSALM 141

TO MAKE YOUR ENEMY FALL ON THEIR OWN SWORD

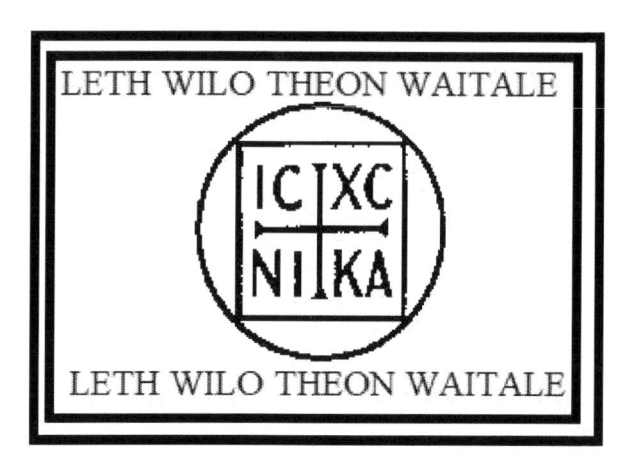

```
LETH WILO THEON WAITALE
    IC┬XC
    NI┴KA
LETH WILO THEON WAITALE
```

Write the above seal on clean parchment during the hour of Mars on a Tuesday and fumigate it with peppercorn. Pray the psalm five times and impale the seal on an iron nail or a small knife to the southside of a nut bearing tree.

PSALM 142

FOR THE RELEASE OF A PRISONER

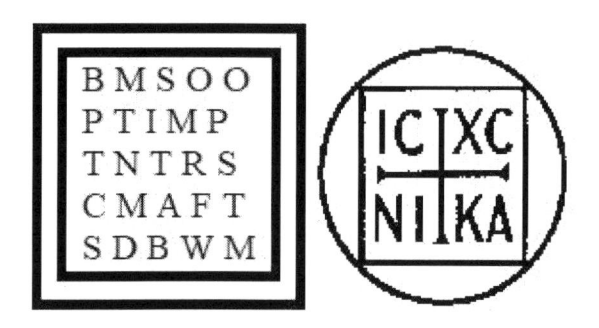

```
B M S O O
P T I M P
T N T R S
C M A F T
S D B W M
```

    IC┬XC
    NI┴KA

Write the above seal on clean parchment on a Sunday during the hour of the Sun and fumigate it with orange. Pray the psalm six times over the seal, and swallow it. Should the prisoner not be doing the work; the individual working for them should burn the seal, rub the ashes into their hand, and visit the prisoner, being sure to touch both their wrists.

PSALM 143

SO THAT YOUR ENEMIES MAY NOT SEE YOU

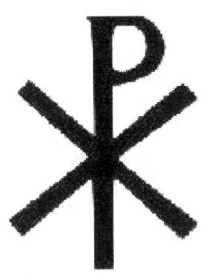

DM. ADONAY. FME. IFUT. THM.

Write the above words on the back page of a small psalter in black ink on Holy Saturday and fumigate it with myrrh while praying the psalm 3 times. Carry the psalter in your pocket.

TO RECEIVE SPIRITUAL WISDOM

```
            ℞
  Teach me to        do thy will;

    ℞        N.N.      ℞

  for thou art        my God
            ℞
```

Write the above seal on calfskin parchment on a Sunday during the hour of Mercury. Fumigate it with marigold and lavender and pray the psalm six times over it. Keep the seal within your prayer book or Bible.

PSALM 144

TO ATTACK YOUR ENEMIES

> Cast forth lightning, and scatter them: shoot out thine arrows, and destroy them

On a Tuesday at dawn, write five slips of paper with the above verse in red ink, after which you shall write the name of your enemy. Roll each seal around a peppercorn and set them in a circle. Pour alcohol over the seals and light them, praying the psalm five times.

TO SILENCE TROUBLESOME STEPCHILDREN

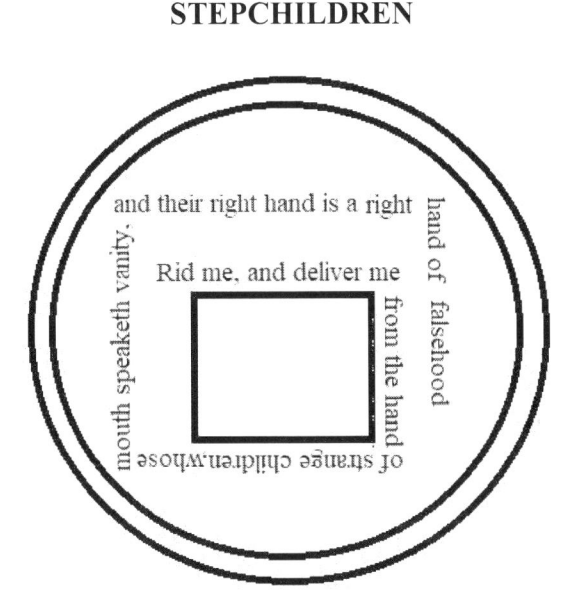

Rid me, and deliver me from the hand of strange children, whose mouth speaketh vanity, and their right hand is a right hand of falsehood

Mark the above seal on aluminum during the hour of Saturn on a Wednesday, writing the initials of the children within the square. Fumigate it with lavender and pray the psalm 8 times over it. Wrap the seal in grey cloth and hide it in a wooden box in a dark place.

PSALM 145

TO DRAW ATTENTION TO YOUR WORK

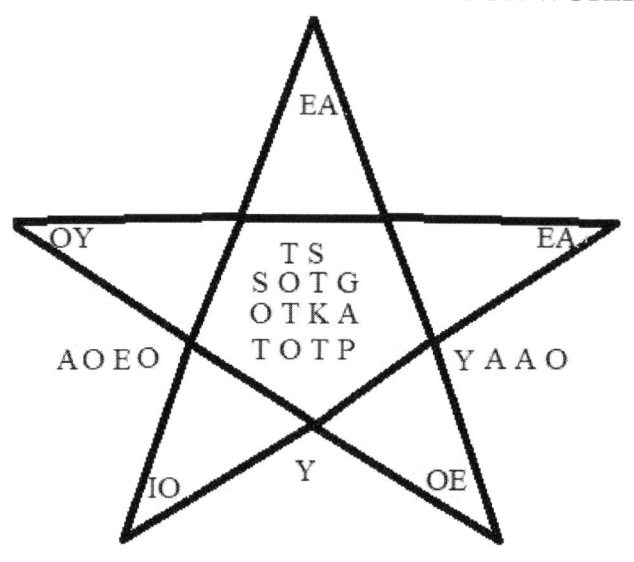

```
         EA
  OY            EA
       T S
      S O T G
      O T K A
 AOEO  T O T P  YAAO
       
    IO    Y    OE
```

Mark the above seal on gold foil in the day and hour of the Sun, the moon increasing; and fumigate it with frankincense while praying the psalm 6 times. Place it over the door of the place of your work.

PSALM 146

FOR EYESIGHT

```
        EOOEEEEYEOEI
ADO          NAI
EOOEEEEYEOEI
OTB          OTE
        EOOEEEEYEOEI
```

Make two of the above seal on gold foil at sunrise on a Sunday and pray the psalm six times over each. Lay them over the eyes of the person and make them keep their eyes closed for six minutes. Repeat daily for six days.

PSALM 147

TO HEAL A BROKEN HEART

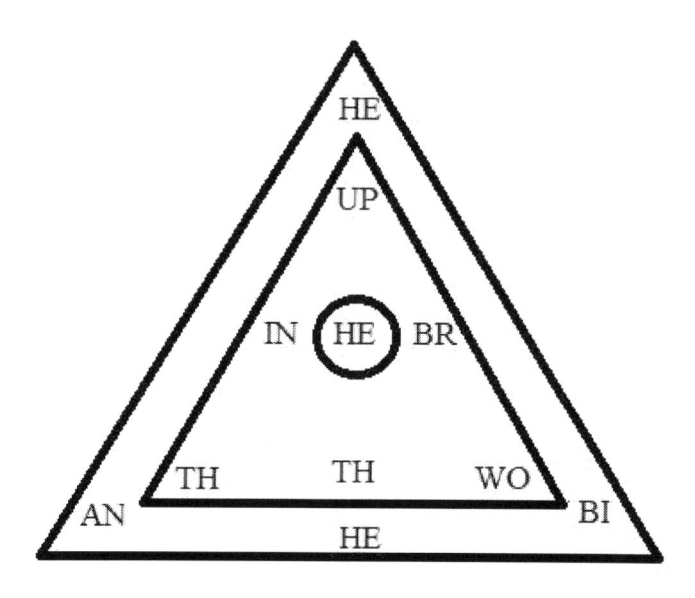

(Triangle seal containing: HE / UP / IN (HE) BR / TH TH WO / AN HE BI)

Mark the above seal on copper during the day and hour of Venus, the moon waxing; and fumigate it with rose. Pray the psalm 7 times over the seal, and wear it near your heart.

TO LEARN STELLAR ARTS

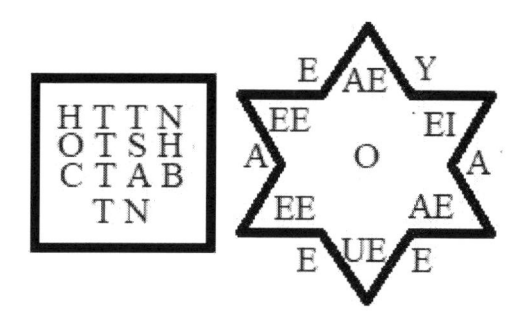

(Square with letters: H T T N / O T S H / C T A B / T N)

(Six-pointed star with letters: E AE Y / EE EI / A O A / EE AE / E UE E)

Make the above square on silver, and the star seal upon the back, during the full moon in the hour of Mercury and fumigate with lavender and camphor. Pray the psalm 8 times over the seal, and wear it during your studies.

PSALM 148

FOR SPECIAL FAVORS

> LETHE PETENA OT ADONAI FEA ATE

Write the above words on clean parchment and attach it to the wick of an oil lamp. Light the lamp and pray the psalm 7 times in honor of the 7 spirits that attend the throne of the Most High.

PSALM 149

TO CATCH A FUGITIVE

Mark the above seal on lead on a Saturday during the hour of Mars, replacing N.N. with the name of the fugitive, and fumigate it with myrrh. Pray the psalm three times over it in honor of the Most Holy Trinity

PSALM 150

TO ASK A SIGN

```
P.Y. ADONAI
P.Y. EL in ZION
AI I I E IAE O I OE
```

Mark the above seal on gold foil at sunrise on a Sunday and pray the psalm three times over it, fumigating it with frankincense. Lay the seal on top of your bible and pray about the matter for which you ask the sign.

FURTHER READING

Black and White Magic of Doctor Corbeaux Volume 1

A collection of spells, recipes, and works based on the original classic "Black and White Magic of Marie Laveau." Includes the significance of cards in divination, the use of candles, psalms, roots, and oils

Black and White Magic of Dr. Corbeaux Volume 2

A collection of works, spells, and recipes for various situations; modeled after the classic "Black and White Magic of Marie Laveau." Included in this volume are rituals with new saints, as well as a form of spider divination.

The Working Girl's Conjure Book: Hoodoo for Hookers

Everyone needs a little conjure in their lives and who more than the industrious working girl? Need protection while out on the job? Want a little something to strum up new business? Need a way to keep the police away? Want to tie down that really rich client? I've got a ritual for that...

SATOR AREPO TENET OPERA ROTAS: Prayers, Rituals, and Charms of Protection, Exorcism, and Uncrossing.

The following text presents a series of rituals, prayers, and charms for the purpose of protection, both physical and spiritual. The reversing of hexes, cleansing, and exorcism prayers will also be discussed.

Handy Human Finger Bones: Haintological Studies Volume 1

Handy Human Finger Bones: Haintological Studies is the first in a series of books where I will discuss subjects involving ghosts, graveyards, and the various beliefs and conjures relating to them. Over the course of these volumes, we will be discussing everything from power hotspots in cemeteries, how to conjure or expel the spirits of the dead, the materia magica of the graveyard, the occult significance of various human bones, and other folklore relating to the spirits of the dead in general.

Cartomancy 2.0: Further Studies in Cartomancy

In 2011 I wrote "Cartomancy; Divination with Playing Cards" (http://www.lulu.com/shop/dr-lazarus-corbeaux/cartomancy-divination-with-playing-cards/paperback/product-17990527.html) as an introductory bare bones extremely basic text on beginning divination with 54 playing cards. I was never really happy with my early books, and I have wanted to publish an update to my cartomancy book, with extended card meanings and spreads. To avoid repetitiveness, I will skip over the preliminary information that I have previously discussed in "Cartomancy; Divination with Playing Cards" and move directly on to the material I wish I had added in the original, as well as other helpful hints I never included in the original book. For those of you who have already read my previous book, you will be aware of the card correspondence regarding various saints and biblical events. In this text, I will include more correspondences, and include information on how the individual practitioner can graft the various spirits or deities they work with into the cards themselves.

Love Conjures: A Collection of Spiritual Works for Love and Relationships

What follows is a collection of recipes, workings, and advice to assist in the working of conjure for love, attraction, fidelity, and control for the use of individuals, both male and female, and of whatever sexual orientation.Before you make use of any of the herbs or materials referenced in this work, make sure you are not allergic. The key to success in conjuring a partner is to never get caught. Tell no one what you're doing, never let anyone see you doing it, and never admit to it. Often, though not always, should your target become aware of what you are doing, your works will falter - whether for psychological suggestion in the mind of the conjured, or through some esoteric principle inherent in love working, no one could say definitively. All I can say, it has been my experience that it is best to never let your target know that they are being, or have been conjured.

Santisima Muerte Trilogy: Altars, Prayers, and Rituals...with added materials

A trilogy of my original three books on the subject of the Santisima Muerte with added materials. Subjects included: how to erect an altar and work with the Santisima Muerte; recipes, rituals, and divination techniques to assist in communication with the saint.

Narco-Conjure Volume 1: Spells, Charms, and Formulas for Drug Dealers

What follows is a collection of prayers, charms, spells, rituals, formulas and folklore that may be of use to the purveyor of fine controlled substances for assistance in their economic endeavors. Need 5.0 off your back? Business too slow? Need some added protection on the street? Got a friend or employee in jail? Need to influence a court case? All this and more will be discussed

Black Magic for Kids: A Beginner's Guide to Hexes

There's no reason hexes, curses, and jinxes have to be complicated. Black Magic for Kids: A Beginner's Guide to Hexes presents a list of rituals, formulas, and prayers that are easily performed by the novice of all ages.

Black Magic for Kids Volume 2

Volume 2 of Black Magic for Kids contains the names, symbols, and rituals for employing the use of various evil spirits for practical purposes. Slightly more complex than Volume 1, but still an easy usable manual for the aspiring practitioner of the black arts.

Pum Pum Conjure: Attracting Women Through Conjure

A collection of charms, spells, and recipes for men to use for the sole purpose of attracting the romantic interests of ladies.

DIVINATION AND SPIRITUAL WORK

Copyright 2019 Dr. Corbeaux

If you would like to contact the author for divination or spiritual work, forward all questions to drcorbeaux@gmail.com

Author Page:
http://www.amazon.com/author/gedelazarus

Printed in Great Britain
by Amazon